Unlocking the Door:
A Key to
Biblical Prophecy

by Dennis J. Woods

HUNTINGTON HOUSE PUBLISHERS

Huntington House Publishers
P.O. Box 53788
Lafayette, Louisiana 70505

Library of Congress Card Catalog Number 94-77034
ISBN 1-56384-039-1

Unless otherwise indicated all Scripture quotations
are taken from the King James Version.

Dedication

In Loving Memory of
Margarete P. Woods
my mother
1928 to 1992

Contents

Preface

In 1976, as a young sailor aboard the *U.S.S. England CG-22*, I read my first Hal Lindsey book. I remember being fascinated with upcoming prophetic events, and ever since then I diligently studied this great subject. I read everything that I could get my hands on until I believed I had a good handle on eschatology.

Some years later, I was stationed in Alameda, California, attached to the Naval Air Station Police, where I used to listen to Dr. Gene Scott, of Wescott Christian Center, in Los Angeles. Dr. Scott was an articulate and outspoken scholar. It was through his ministry that I learned a great deal about the major and minor prophets concerning the "end times."

After leaving the navy in 1982, I moved to Hawaii, where I lived in the small town of Lihue on the island of Kauai. There I received my first Clarence Larkin book. Mr. Larkin's writings took me even further into this intriguing subject. As I read his book on the Revelation of Jesus Christ, it seemed as though I had graduated into the advanced class. Sometime after that I also read his books, *Dispensational Truth* and *Daniel*.

Although the authors I've mentioned thus far are all doctrinal proponents of the pre-tribulation position, I hadn't really taken a doctrinal position at that time. My reading was still driven by a fascination with the authors and the subject. There were some deep uncertainties in my mind about the "pre-trib" theories, but I just couldn't put my finger on them in my still immature understanding.

Many years had elapsed, and I now was in ministry and recently ordained, though working in the security field as the head of security of Luster Products of Chicago. I was making rounds one day, and the Lord spoke to me and said, "He can't get out." I thought to myself, *He can't get out*? The Spirit then brought the Scripture to my remembrance: The beast ascends out of the bottomless pit, and unless he's let loose, he can't get out!

At that point I didn't realize I would be writing a book. I hadn't even made the connection between doctrine and the revelation the Lord had given me. Then one day, while reading 2 Thessalonians, chapter 2—a passage with which I had been familiar for years—it hit me: *he who now letteth*. Right away I recalled that Satan was to be cast in the bottomless pit by an angel who held the key to the pit. I began to research this thoroughly, and then it all connected. I saw that the "he who now letteth" was an angel, not the Holy Spirit as conjectured by the best minds in the pre-trib debate.

If the "he" is not the Holy Spirit as many suppose, then how does that affect pre-trib theory? Then I mused, if the pre-trib theory is wrong, what is at stake? Millions of unsuspecting and inadequately prepared Christians are what's at stake. What if a whole generation of Christians *do* enter the seventieth week of Daniel?

After studying some of the best minds on the subject

of eschatology and pre-trib doctrine, such as Larkin, Lindsey, Pentecost, Walvoord, and many others, I present to you *Unlocking the Door: A Key to Biblical Prophecy.* Although I am not a theologian, I hope you will find that this work is quite scholarly. You will find it is based entirely on the Bible, with many references in both Old and New Testaments. It is quite practical from a biblical point of view; there are no wild assumptions, as you find in a lot of pre-trib doctrine.

It should be noted that I have the highest respect for the authors that I mentioned above and embrace them as fellow yokemen of the Gospel. I say this up front because I am rather hard on their doctrinal positions in this book, but I do not intend this harshness to extend to them as individuals, or to anyone else who agrees with them. Offending my Christian brothers and sisters is not the object of this book. Enjoy what the Lord has given me.

My thanks to the Lord Jesus Christ who supplied all of my needs according to His riches in glory.

Acknowledgments

Be it known to all, Lord Jesus Christ strategically placed each one of the following, named individuals in my life to help me when I could not have helped myself. These servants of God, friends, and associates were all instrumental in my growth as a person, a Christian, and a minister. Without their care, love, and instruction, I could not have come as far as I have. May the Lord Jesus Christ continue to bless them all richly.

Bishop William and Rose McCoy, Am I My Brother's Keeper, Inc., Harvey/Chicago, Illinois; Pastor Annie P. Whitted, Faith and Deliverance Church, Harvey, Illinois; Pastor Effie Gant, The Highway Byway Apostolic Ministry; Bishop Leonard Rimpson, Fellowship Church of God in Christ Apostolic, Joliet, Illinois; Elder Alexander Clark; Elder Ron Anderson and Pastor Bean, The Universal House of Prayer, Chicago, Illinois; Harold Mark Austin, my dear brother in Christ; Evangelist Theresa Darling,

Faith and Deliverance Church; Pastor Fernando Rivas, Chicago Victory Center, Chicago, Illinois; Pastor Joey Rivas, St. Louis Power House Ministries, St. Louis, Missouri; Evangelist Louise Hunter, The Love and Charity Homeless Shelter, Racine, Wisconsin; Deacon James Ray Woods (for all of your support and prayers); my friends at the 700 Club, Chicago; Ms. Kawana Laray (you never stopped praying); Mr. and Mrs. Hawkins, of WWHN Radio Chicago, Illinois; Lydia Graham (keep on singing); Dr. Arthur M. Brazier, Apostolic Church of God, Chicago, Illinois; my dear friends at the Milwaukee Rescue Mission (MRM) Spiritual Program, spring, summer, and fall 1993; Bob Murray (for his computer assistance and moral support); Pastor Patrick and Barbara Vanderburgh, Pastor L. Bowman, Pastor Tom Griffey, all of MRM; my first students, who helped and challenged me, Benito Olivas, Jeff Caupp, Nate Spate, and Kenneth Shaw, MRM; Pastor Gregory Flood, and the congregation of the Allen Chapel A.M.E. Church, Milwaukee, Wisconsin; Darryl and Valerie Woodley, MRM, for all of the fellowship and encouragement; special thanks to the Luster family, of Luster Products, Chicago, Illinois: Fred Luster, Sr. (1991); Jory Luster; Freddie Luster, Jr.; Sonja Luster; Precious Luster, and Herbert Luster.

It should be noted that those in the list above do not necessarily endorse the views of the author.

Introduction

Over the past several years, I have embarked on a comprehensive study of eschatology and the diverse viewpoints held by the Christian community concerning the rapture of the church. As defined, the word *rapture* means to be "caught up," or the transporting of a person from one place to another, particularly into heaven itself. It should be noted that the word *rapture* does not appear in our authorized version of the Bible, but such an event is implied in both Old and New Testaments.

The rapture of the church is also known as the translation of the saints. During the translation of the saints, the Christians will instantaneously receive their immortal bodies at the coming of the Lord. References to this can be found in many scriptural passages; however, the main ones are 1 Corinthians 15:42-55, 1 Thessalonians 4:15-18, and Philippians 3:21.

When one takes an analytical approach to studying

this great event, confusion may result. As we will see later in this chapter, there are at least four premillennial theories on when the rapture might occur. In each case, the relationship to the seventieth week of Daniel's prophecy to the occurrence of the rapture—whether prior to it, during it, or after it—is where the controversy lies.

Grappling with the different exegetical approaches to this takes some doing. For example, when on the prophetic calendar does this event take place? The Bible says that the day and the hour are known only to God and not revealed to man.

Although the timing of the rapture has been kept secret, it has not prevented many from claiming to know when it would occur, bringing about countless erroneous predictions. Invariably, they're proved wrong by the mere fact that it doesn't occur on the day they predicted. All of this inconsistency has added to the existing confusion.

On the other hand, there are the divergent schools of thought held by the Christian denominations on when the rapture occurs. As a result, and unfortunately, a lot of name calling and strife have emerged as the dominant manner of dialogue. The student of eschatology must navigate through a turbulent sea of opposing doctrines and cast his line for the theory with the least bones.

Why the wide range of positions on when the rapture occurs? Well, I guess, just as there are differences in people and their opinions, there will certainly be differences in how they interpret the Scriptures. In some cases, different opinions can be useful in interpreting Scriptures; one may clearly see a point that another has overlooked. Just as the passage in Proverbs says, "In a multitude of counsellors there is safety."

This can be seen in all four of the gospels. Each author writes from a different perspective concerning the life of the Lord Jesus Christ. For example, in the Gospel according to Matthew, Jesus' ancestry is traced back to Abraham and David. Matthew also focuses upon Jesus' lineage and identity as the "Covenanted King," the son of David.

In the Gospel of Mark, the author centers more on Jesus' deeds as Jehovah's righteous servant, the "Branch." In this gospel, many of Jesus' miracles are recorded. In the book of Luke, Jesus' humanity and role as the Son of man is the theme, and roots are traced back to Adam. Jesus does a lot of parabolic teaching in this great gospel.

Then finally, in the Gospel according to John, we find that Jesus was the "Word of God," or the *logos*, who was manifested in the flesh. Jesus was indeed all God and all man; therefore, John's focus was the deity of Christ.

Now from these four gospels we get a complete and very dynamic account of this man Jesus Christ. None of the gospels should ever be regarded as more authoritative than the other, and it is in this harmony that we are given a wealth of revelation of the God-Man, Jesus Christ. We have a better understanding of our Lord and Savior.

Now, as we continue to look at the life of Jesus Christ from the perspective of the synoptic gospels, we can see that there was a lot of uncertainty as to who Jesus was, even in those days. Men differed in their opinions, leading to quite a controversy. A good illustration of this is found in Matthew 16:13-17. Peter was asked by Jesus, Who do men say that I am? Peter replied, Some say John the Baptist, some say Elijah, and some say Jeremiah. This account reveals how diverse opinion was regarding Jesus, and how sincere people were, and yet this did not prevent them from being *wrong*.

Jesus queried Peter further, Who do you say that I am? Peter replied, Thou are the Christ, the Son of God, and Jesus said, Blessed art thou, for flesh and blood have not revealed this to you, but my father in heaven has. Revelation of Christ comes from God, far exceeding anything that man's wisdom could ever comprehend or know.

Although speculating and proposing opinions are a normal result of processing information, when it comes to things pertaining to the kingdom of God, without the illumination of the Holy Spirit, man's perceptions and opinions will never attain God's truth. As people, we are limited to finite reasoning, which often leads to misinterpretations and doctrinal error.

Therefore, 1 Corinthians 2:10-14, tells us God, through the Holy Spirit, reveals things pertaining to the kingdom of God which would otherwise be impossible to know. "But the natural man receiveth not the things of the Spirit of God: for they are foolishness unto Him" (1 Cor. 2:14). Where there is no revelation from God, we are limited to the opinions and interpretations of others; even the scholars must rely upon available exposition, commentaries, and exegesis. Historical research and archaeological finds are also helpful, but even these have their limitations.

For this reason, interpreting the Scriptures can be problematic, considering the varying schools of thought on practically any doctrinal subject. This has caused much strife in the body of Christ and even the split of churches and whole denominations. As I mentioned earlier, there are different positions prevalent in most Christian circles concerning the rapture of the church. Of these are four premillennial views which I would like to summarize.

Probably the most prevalent rapture theory is the *Pretribulation Rapture Theory*. This theory is based on a literal hermeneutical interpretation of both Old and New Testament Scriptures which address eschatological events. The tenets of this doctrine are: (a) The church will not go through any part of the seventieth week of Daniel and is raptured up PRIOR to the seventieth week; (b) God has two distinct programs for the "church" and for Israel (According to this doctrine, the tribulation is the time of Jacob's [Israel's] trouble, not the church.); (c) The church must be raptured up before the revealing of the Antichrist which is based on 2 Thessalonians, chapter 2. Again, these are just a few of this doctrine's tenets, and this is not a complete list.

The next theory on the rapture is the *Mid-tribulation Rapture Theory*. The basic tenets of this doctrine are centered around the sounding of the "seventh trumpet" found in Revelation, chapter 11. This doctrine holds to the rapture occurring *midway* through the seventieth week, correlating the seventh trumpet (Rev. 11:18) with the "last trumpet" of 1 Corinthians 15:52.

The next theory on the rapture is the *Partial Rapture Theory*. This theory states that not all of the church will be ready to be raptured at the coming of the Lord and utilizes elements of the pre-trib theory but contends that not all of the church will be ready to be raptured when the Lord comes, prior to the seventieth week. Therefore, the Lord raptures the church in different segments.

The final rapture theory is that of the *Post Rapture Theory*. This theory states that Christ's second advent and the rapture of the church will happen at the same time, both occurring at the end of the seventieth week of Daniel.

From these four theories and other little known doctrines, the student of prophecy must inevitably affiliate with one of these positions. Although one's understanding of prophecy will not affect one's salvation status, practically all Christian churches have embraced one of these doctrinal points of view, which leads us to another very important question. What difference does it make? Well, believe it or not, it could have a lot of influence on one's manner of Christian living. I will be examining that question in detail in the final chapter of this book.

As I said before, the rapture theory to which you prescribe probably won't make or break you. However, what is important is that we believe that Jesus Christ is the Son of God, born of the virgin Mary, who went about doing good and healing those who were oppressed by the devil. He was crucified for the sins of the world. He died and rose again on the third day, and is alive and seated at the right hand of God. He is also the Head of the Church, which is His Body, and is currently our Mediator, our High Priest, and our Advocate. In Him alone, by the shedding of His blood, have we salvation and eternal life. The Lord shall return for His glorious church and change our vile forms and fashion us to be like His glorious body.

Now, upon *these* tenets there are no valid opinions of men. If this is what your faith is based upon, then on this we certainly can agree. Just as the Bible states: There is no other name under heaven given among men whereby we must be saved! When the Lord returns for the true Church, those of us who are born again shall be "caught up" to meet Him in the air.

None of this has any connection to rapture doctrine, you believe, so there should be no judgments made regarding one's salvation in light of their eschatological position. Only love should reign.

It is this author's intention to share with you what the Lord has given to me on this great subject. I'm not claiming to be the only one with God's truth, but it is my deepest desire that you understand what I have to say on this issue, and that it be a blessing to you. Although this is a complicated subject, I will attempt to address the basic elements of end time doctrine so that even beginners will be able to comprehend it.

One

༺༺ ༒༒

Daniel the Prophet

Of the four major prophets found in the Old Testament, the book of Daniel is the smallest in size. However, in its twelve chapters, Daniel probably has more significant eschatological writings than the others. This makes the book indispensable. Without it, the book of Revelation would be even a greater mystery. There is extremely important information found in Daniel which cannot be found in any other book of the Bible, such as vital revelation concerning the seventieth week and information pertaining to the Gentile world powers, as depicted in King Nebuchadnezzar's dream.

Many liken Daniel's writings to a prophetic key. I believe this observation is true, because without Daniel's prophecies, one could not unlock the understanding to many of God's prophetic truths. To get a glimpse of the use of this prophetic key, let's examine a passage of Scripture found in Matthew 24.

Here we find that the Lord is telling His disciples about the times and condition of the world shortly before His second advent. Beginning at verse 14, the passage says:

> And this Gospel of the kingdom shall be preached in all the world for a witness unto all nations; and then shall the end come. When ye therefore shall see the abomination of desolation, spoken of by Daniel the prophet, stand in the holy place (whoso readeth, let him understand). (Matt. 24:14-15)

In these passages Jesus provides some insight on events to come. In verse 14, we see that the gospel of the kingdom must be preached in all the world before the end can come. Then, in verse 15, Jesus speaks of a prophetic event called the abomination of desolation. The Lord also refers us to Daniel the prophet, saying: let him who reads understand.

Since Jesus refers us to Daniel, it is proof to those who ascribe to His authority that Daniel's prophecies are absolutely indispensable to any student of prophecy. And, those who deny His authority are, nonetheless, affected by them. Through Daniel, we understand a great deal about the beast and his kingdom. We must be thoroughly acquainted with the events of Daniel in order to go on.

Babylonian Captivity

In approximately 597 B.C., the city of Jerusalem was besieged by King Nebuchadnezzar, and the Jews were taken back to Babylon as slaves. The king then issued an edict that all of the Jews of noble lineage, without blemish, and who were skillful in all wisdom and knowledge, would be set apart for service in the king's court.

Daniel was one of the young men chosen for this duty. Because God had gifted Daniel with great intellectual skills, he proved to be a real asset to King Nebuchadnezzar, particularly because Daniel could interpret visions and dreams. As a result of these gifts, God gave Daniel great favor with King Nebuchadnezzar. Daniel's prophecies (via the king's dreams) foretold the times we are beginning to witness now in these last days. Of particular concern was the identity of the ruler of the final Gentile kingdom who would lead the earth into the most horrendous period of time ever experienced by the human race, called the Great Tribulation.

King Nebuchadnezzar's Dream

In the second chapter of the book of Daniel, we find that the king had a terrifying dream which awakened him out of his sleep. The king then summoned all of his astrologers, magicians, wise men, and sorcerers to quiz them on the interpretation of the dream. The king instructed his mystic cabinet that if they were able to interpret the dream, he would reward them handsomely. If they were not able to accomplish his directive, they would be killed and their houses and possessions destroyed. Well, obviously these men protested and told the king that his request was impossible to satisfy. All of their lives were threatened, including Daniel's.

After hearing about the king's edict, Daniel and his three companions convened and prayed to God for the interpretation of the dream to be revealed to them, and God answered with an analysis of the entire dream. Let's examine the passage:

> Thou, O king, sawest, and behold a great image. This great image, whose brightness was excellent, stood before thee; and the form thereof was terrible. This image's head was of fine gold, his breast and his arms of silver, his belly and his thighs of brass, His legs of iron, his feet part of iron, part of clay. Thou sawest till that a stone was cut out without hands, which smote the image upon his feet that were of iron and clay, and brake them to pieces. (Dan. 2:31-34)

The Metallic Man

The king saw a great image, a monstrous man whose body was composed of four different metals. The head was made of fine gold, and his breast and arms were made of silver; his belly and thighs were made of brass, and his legs were made of iron, while his feet were made of iron and clay. Then, according to verses 34 and 35, a stone was cut without the use of hands and struck the image on the feet, completely destroying it. This same stone became a mountain and filled the whole earth. This is the terrible dream the king had forgotten until Daniel's revelation.

Daniel proceeds to give the interpretation of the king's dream. He assigns the king as the head of gold, characterizing the kingdom of Babylon. After Babylon, another kingdom, inferior to her, would rise (the silver breast and arms), representing the Medo-Persian Empire. After the Medo-Persian Empire, another would rise which is the belly and thighs of brass. This is the Grecian Empire. Finally, the last kingdom to rise was that of the iron legs, the Roman Empire.

According to Daniel, the kingdom of iron would arrive on the world scene in two different phases; one was ancient Rome (the leg of iron), and the other will appear in a reconstructed version, believed by many to come into power soon. This kingdom is said to consist of feet made of iron and clay; they shall be partly strong and partly brittle. However, just as iron and clay cannot cleave together, neither will this divided kingdom adhere one to the other.

The fact that this kingdom is yet future is addressed in verse 44, which says:

> And in the days of these kings [the ten toes], shall the God of heaven set up a kingdom, which shall never be destroyed: and the kingdom shall not be left to another people, but it shall break into pieces and consume all these kingdoms, and it shall stand forever. (Dan. 2:44)

Now in this interpretation of the dream, the Lord gives us a course in world history. Another interesting facet of these passages is that it shows the decline in splendor of world rule, represented by the devaluating metals. For example, silver is worth less than gold, and brass less than silver, and iron less than brass. Yet, while these kingdoms may have been decreasing in splendor, they were certainly increasing in military strength. Silver is stronger than gold; brass is stronger than silver, and iron is stronger than brass.

The last empire was the ten-toed kingdom which shall be in power at the time of the Lord's return. Although this kingdom shall be as strong as iron, it shall also be as weak as clay. This ten-toed kingdom shall consist of two opposing elements (iron and clay), causing serious internal conflict. The final element of this great vision, is the stone, which is Jesus Christ Himself, the chief cornerstone.

The Jews rejected Christ during His first advent (Acts 4:10-12), and between His two advents, Jesus was going to build His church (Matt. 16:18) until the fullness of the Gentile church comes in (Rom. 11:25). Then shall the Lord set up His Davidic Kingdom during His millennial reign here on the earth.

In Luke 21, Jesus makes reference to the Gentile control over Jerusalem; the passage says:

> And they shall fall by the edge of the sword, and shall be led away captive into all nations: and Jerusalem shall be trodden down of the Gentiles, until the times of the Gentiles be fulfilled. (Luke 21:24)

The "times of the Gentiles" began with the Babylonian captivity and will close under the domination of the ten-toed kingdom, shown in Daniel, chapter 2. Although Israel has been re-established as a nation since 1948, and is autonomous, Jerusalem shall go back into captivity, according to the prophet Zechariah (Zech. 14:2), under the authority of the ten-toed kingdom for forty-two months (Rev. 11:1-2).

Daniel's Vision of the Four Beasts

In the seventh chapter of Daniel, the prophet has a vision of four monstrous beasts which pertain to the same kingdoms revealed to King Nebuchadnezzar in his dream. Beginning at verse 4, we see that the first beast was like a lion which had an eagle's wings; this coincides with the head of gold (Babylon) in chapter 2. The second beast was like a bear, which had three ribs in its mouth and devoured much flesh, coinciding with the arms and breast of silver and the Medo-Persian Empire. The next beast was like a leopard, with four wings; this coincides with the belly and thighs of brass (Greece).

After these, Daniel sees a beast so indescribable he could think of no animal with which to compare it. This beast was terrible and exceedingly strong, having great iron teeth, but this beast was different from the others in that it had ten horns! This beast coincides with the iron legs of Rome, and the ten horns coincide with the ten toes of iron and clay.

Daniel then tells us that while he was considering the ten horns, there came up among them another little horn, which plucked out three of the other horns by the roots. The prophet recounts that this little horn had eyes like a man and a mouth speaking great things. In verse 17, Daniel begins his interpretation of the vision and tells us that these beasts are four kings who shall rise out of the earth. Then, in verses 19-25, he shifts his focus to the fourth king. In verse 23, Daniel gives us some important information:

> The fourth beast shall be the fourth kingdom upon the earth, which shall be diverse from all kingdoms, and shall devour the whole earth, and tread it down, and break it into pieces. And the ten horns [ten toes, see Dan. 2:42] out of this kingdom are ten kings that shall arise: and another shall rise after them; and he shall be diverse from the first. (Dan. 7:23-24)

Daniel is clear that this little horn shall rise after the ten horns rise, and the ten horns shall proceed out of the fourth beast, which I believe is Rome. The ten-horned kingdom and the ten-toed kingdom are the same. They both represent the reconstructed Roman Empire. According to verse 25, when this little horn rises, it will begin its rule with speaking out against God. We are also told that this little horn shall make war with the saints for a time (*id-dawn*, Hebrew for "one year"), times (two years), and the dividing of time (one-half year), which totals three-and-one-half years.

After this little horn begins its tyrannical and blasphemous three-and-one-half-year reign on the earth, it shall be destroyed by "God's wrath" (See Dan. 7:11,26; 9:27; and Rev. 19:20.). Yes, this little horn shall be a man who rules the ten-nation allegiance, blasphemes God, and makes war with the saints. This man is also known as the son of perdition (2 Thess. 2:4) and the beast (Rev. 13). An in-depth study of this tyrant comes in a later chapter.

Daniel's Seventy Weeks

Since the beginning of the Jewish captivity in Babylon, Daniel lived under the rules of the Babylonian and Medo-Persian empires. King Nebuchadnezzar ruled until approximately 562 B.C. His grandson, Belshazzar, took over the Babylonian throne in about 556 B.C. and ruled until he was slain in 539 B.C. Then Darius the Mede was made the ruler over the Chaldeans under the universal monarchy of Cyrus. It was Cyrus who was responsible for welding together the forces of the Medes and the Persians.

The prophet Isaiah prophesied some one hundred and fifty years before Cyrus' birth that he would order the rebuilding of the temple in Jerusalem (Isa. 44:28). For seventy long years, the Jews were in captivity in Babylon under the Chaldeans, the Medes and the Persians, prophesied by Jeremiah in 25:11.

Daniel knew the time of captivity was about to end and prayed that God would fulfill the time of their captivity (Dan. 9:3-23). Now, while Daniel was in prayer, the angel Gabriel came to give Daniel understanding concerning the seventy weeks. Let's take a look at what the angel had to say to Daniel, beginning with verse 24:

> Seventy weeks are determined upon thy people and upon thy holy city, to finish the transgression, and to make an end of sins, and to make reconciliation for iniquity, and to bring everlasting righteousness, and to seal up the vision and prophecy, and to anoint the most Holy. (Dan. 9:24)

Notice that Gabriel redirects Daniel's attention away from the seventy years of Babylonian captivity to a time period that will consist of seventy weeks of years. During this time, God will bring about his entire agenda, outlined in verse 24. The word *week* comes from the Hebrew word *sheb-oo-aw*, which literally means "sevened", that is, a week, specifically, of years. Just as a normal week has seven days, these weeks have seven years in them. For example, when Jacob had to serve Laban for seven years in order to marry Rachel, Genesis 29:28 states that "Jacob did so, and fulfilled her 'week'." Therefore, in a 490-year period (7 years times 70 weeks of years), God would finish His divine agenda. However, these weeks of years do not run consecutively but are broken up in three segments. Let's take a look at the passage:

> Know therefore and understand, that from the going forth of the commandment to restore and to build Jerusalem unto the Messiah the Prince shall be seven weeks, and threescore and two weeks: the street shall be built again, and the wall, even in troublous times. And after threescore and two weeks shall Messiah be cut off, but not for himself: and the people of the prince that shall come shall destroy the city and the sanctuary; and the end thereof shall be flood, and unto the end of the war desolations are determined. (Dan. 9:25-26)

The first segment is found in verse 25, which refers to the restoration and rebuilding of Jerusalem. Although it was Cyrus who first announced the rebuilding of the Jewish temple, it was actually King Artaxerxes who gave the permission for the city and the temple to be rebuilt in 444 B.C. (Neh. 2:1-8). In this seven-week (forty-nine years) period, this prophecy was fulfilled.

In the second segment, verse 26, we begin to count sixty-two weeks, or 434 years, from the rebuilding of the temple. However it is important to note that this prophecy of Messiah to be cut off was after the sixty-two weeks (434 years), not before or within it. Also, according to this prophetic segment, after the sixty and two weeks was the destruction of Jerusalem and the temple, which was done in A.D. 70 by Titus Flavius Vespasianus, Emperor of Rome. So this brings us to sixty-nine fulfilled prophetic weeks, totaling 483 years, which are already fulfilled.

The Seventieth Week

In verse 27, we find this passage gives us a wealth of prophetic information concerning the third segment, the last remaining week.

> And he shall confirm a covenant with many for one week: and in the midst of the week he shall cause the sacrifice and the oblation to cease, and for the overspreading of abominations he shall make it desolate, even until the consummation, and that determined shall be poured upon the desolate. (Dan. 9:27)

This final week on God's prophetic calendar has been on hold since A.D. 70, when the temple was destroyed by the Romans. It is this week that is surrounded by a lot of controversy, particularly when it comes to the rapture of the Church. The pre-tribers say that the rapture of the Church will occur prior to the arrival of this prophetic week, a position based mainly on the 2 Thessalonians, chapter 2 passage concerning the revealing of the son of perdition, *a.k.a.* Anti-christ, or the beast. They also consider the whole seventieth week as the "wrath of God" to which the Bible says we the Church are not appointed (1 Thess. 5:9).

Then there are the mid-tribers who say the rapture will occur in the middle of the seventieth week and the post-tribers who say that the rapture will occur at the end of the seventieth week.

You can see why the seventieth week is at the center of the rapture controversy, no matter what doctrine one professes. Remember that, no matter what their view of the time frame of the rapture, all of these believe that the seventieth week is yet to come, and most believe that it will be relatively soon.

So, the most important question remains: Will the Church witness the revealing of the Anti-christ and be present when the seventieth week arrives? Many say no. In opposition to this position, I intend to *prove* that this pre-trib doctrine is wrong and has the potential to be very dangerous. Further, I believe it could have devastating effects on millions of unsuspecting Christians, all over the world.

Two

The World Is Preparing for Anti-christ

In Matthew 24, Jesus describes the condition of the world prior to His return to the earth, known as His second advent.

> And ye shall hear of wars and rumors of wars: see that ye be not troubled: for all these things must come to pass, but the end is not yet. For nation shall rise against nation, and kingdom against kingdom: and there shall be famines, and pestilences, and earthquakes, in divers places. All these are the beginning of sorrows. (Matt. 24:6-8)

In Jesus' description of the pre-second advent earth, He used a Greek term that was commonly used to describe a pregnant woman's birth pangs: *o-deen*. As any expecting mother can tell you, the contractions and the pangs she experiences increase in frequency and intensity as the delivery date approaches. The word *o-deen* is the perfect way to convey to us that the signs of Jesus' return will be an increase in the frequency of wars, earthquakes, and pestilences throughout the world. Hence the beginning of *sorrows*, o-deen.

Since the beginning of human history, millions of people have perished due to natural catastrophes, such as killer earthquakes, storms, volcanic eruptions, and great famines. All one would have to do is pick up a newspaper, or watch the evening news, and see that all these are certainly on the increase. I'm sure that the year 1993 will never be forgotten by those who live in the mid-western region of the United States, as the banks of the Mississippi River overflowed. Millions of acres of land were flooded causing damage that ranged in the billions of dollars. On the other end of the scale of tragedy, raging fires swept through southern California, destroying more thousands of acreage and nearly a thousand homes. We also witnessed the effects of a killer earthquake in India, which killed over twenty thousand people, as well as the earthquake that jolted southern California in January 1994.

Other than natural catastrophes, Jesus also mentioned that wars and ethnic conflicts would also be on the increase. Since the beginning of human history there have been wars, but the great wars of this century have caused the greatest loss of life. World Wars I and II, the Vietnam and Korean conflicts, and many other minor (regional) skirmishes (e.g., Afghanistan, Bosnia, etc.) have reeked great carnage. The emotional and financial trauma suffered by the world's nations as a result of these troublesome times has had a devastating effect on international stability. Therefore, organizations such as the United Nations now attempt to devise solutions to these mounting international problems by focusing on their quest for the evasive, magical key to lasting worldwide peace.

Another interesting element of international instability has been the advent of the technological explosion, particularly in the area of military armament. With the introduction of the nuclear bomb, all the world's governments, as well as the earth's populace, are concerned about nuclear war. For the first time in world history, man has the capability to destroy the earth. With the introduction of nuclear and other highly technical weaponry, mass destruction is just a push button away—yes, the hands on the proverbial "Doom's Day Clock" are closing in on the midnight hour.

Out of an extreme sense of urgency, nations try to introduce all manners of bans and limitation treaties in an attempt to halt the proliferation of modern weaponry. There is much concern in the international community that nuclear weapons might fall into the hands of some crazed terrorist who would love to be the catalyst in a nuclear war between nations.

Nuclear war is not the only pressing issue. The nations are equally concerned about the disintegrating social, ethnic, and economic conditions in which they find their own peoples. International—and interracial—relationships are being stressed to maximum capacity. Crime in major cities has now spread into suburban areas as well, reaching frightening epidemic proportions. Unemployment, depression brought on by hopelessness, budget cuts, scandal, waste, embezzlement, drugs, organized crime, and corporate corruption are all symptoms of a sin-sick society.

Social ills have reached an intolerable level; we are not safe anywhere anymore. But, we are not alone; these social pestilences are not just indigenous to the United States but are now becoming international issues at every level of human existence. Every country in the world is hard-pressed to find the solutions to their social and political ills.

Keeping the current condition of the world in mind, we look back to the Bible and find that God's Word predicted such problems. For example, in 2 Timothy 3:1, Paul writes, "This know also, that in the last days perilous times shall come." Jesus said, ". . . and upon the earth distress of nations, with perplexity" (Luke 21:25).

With critical problems so far-flung, facing every nation, common cause and the dire need for a solution are stimulating the world's governments to overcome adversity and unite in this endeavor. No matter what the political or philosophical differences between the nations are, we all share the same planet. We are a global community, suffering practically the same social problems threatening all our safety and our existences, and we are becoming more attuned to international conflicts. Now, when we speak of international and geo-political problems, one region of the world comes to mind as potentially the most volatile—the Middle East.

As we are all aware, the Middle East possesses one of the earth's richest oil supplies. Arabs, Persians, and Africans maintain the majority of control over these vast resources, on which every nation in the world either directly or indirectly depends. Subsequently, these predominantly Islamic nations, which make up a thirteen-nation oil cartel called OPEC, hold in their hands massive political power. Whatever issue the members of OPEC deem important, they have little problem making their wishes known to a world community in need of their petroleum products. Although these Islamic nations have experienced their share of infighting, they joined forces in 1948 against the intrusion of an unwanted neighbor who moved into the region, forever changing the face of the Middle East.

The Emergence of Israel

On 14 May 1948, the Jewish state of Israel was established. Since her formation, Israel's presence in the Middle East has been the single most irritating thorn in the side of every Islamic country. Israeli reclamation of territories given to them by God, particularly Jerusalem and Palestine, has evinced great stress and political hatred in the land.

Further, Israeli annexations and settlements in Palestine, the Western Bank, and Gaza Strip critically upset the balance of this already troubled region. The displacement of millions of Palestinians was widely condemned in the Islamic community and beyond.

Along with Israeli occupation came war with the Jews battling many nations, including Syria, Egypt, Jordan, and Lebanon. Collectively, the Islamic world declared *jihad* (holy war) against Israel, contesting Israel's right to exist in the region. Nation after nation has tried to mediate, pushing the parties just so far in peace treaties of every shape and color; but, to date, nothing has ever lasted. As late as early 1994, Israel and the PLO were carrying on what the media called promising peace talks; but the question remains: will there be a successful peace *solution?*

In light of these and many more international issues, the world is being propelled into an increasingly perplexing situation as it staggers down the road to destruction. We all heave a collective sigh (or groan) in our desire for world peace. Such a craving is understandable; still, it is one of the major catalysts behind the push for the dominance of the humanistic view: that man, not God, will find the solutions to war, pollution, crime, economics, and political unrest.

This line of thinking will result in the world coming together as one. Remember the song, "We Are the World"? The lyrics in that song suggested that man holds the keys to the brighter days to come. Likewise, the hope for a lasting peace is on the agenda of the New World Order, where mankind and his technologies will supply the solutions for which the world has been searching. Man will deliver the world from its troubles. This is the manner in which secular society searches for the answers to the world's problems. The question is: Is the world being lulled into a sense of false hope in man's ability to save the world from impending destruction? As the prophet Jeremiah states, "Cursed be the man that trusteth in man, and maketh flesh his arm, and whose heart departeth from the Lord" (Jer. 17:5).

Our nation, as well as the rest of the international community, slips further and further away from the principles of Jesus Christ, and judgment rapidly approaches. Abominable and sinful behavior practiced by most of the world is accepted as natural, ethnically pure, and the right thing to do. All these evils are perpetuated by the global mass media, stimulating an attitude of acceptance, hence the cliché, "Live for the here and now." Situational ethics (another buzz word), encourages people—in particular, the world's youth who are thus indoctrinated daily—to do whatever they want, because the ends justify the means.

A perfect example of this is legalized abortion. Clearly this practice is murder, but the situational ethic leaves room for redefining the behavior to mean something good. The result is that the most dangerous place for America's children is the mother's womb! Since *Roe v. Wade*, over 30 million babies have been murdered—yet, it's not called murder. Rather, the crime is done in the name of "freedom of choice." This twisted rationale is heralded as one of the fullest expressions of human rights, therefore politically correct and legalized.

The prophet Isaiah stated: "Woe unto them that call evil good, and good evil . . ." (Isa. 5:20). Truly, in man's conquest for self-determination and freedom, the people of the world have actually become slaves to their own evil practices. As James states, "From whence come wars and fightings among you? come they not hence, even of your lusts that war in your members?" (James 4:1).

So when we look at all the presenting issues, we face another question. Who will lead the world *off* of the path to destruction? And, who will have the final say in the international agenda and conquest for peace?

As the world searches for the answers, an important factor must be considered. First of all, there really are only two kingdoms at war here on earth and in the heavenly realms—the kingdom of light and the kingdom of darkness. The kingdom of light, or the kingdom of God, is the kingdom that produced the Savior of mankind, Jesus Christ the Son of God, who shed His blood on Calvary's cross and saved us from certain judgment and the wrath of God to come. Since God is holy and judicious, He must judge sin; therefore, He commands sinners to turn from their evil deeds and repent. Because men love darkness rather than light, the world rejects Jesus Christ, who is mankind's only hope.

On the other hand, there is the kingdom of darkness, ruled by the devil, or Satan. This kingdom of evil operates on a sin and self-interest agenda, by which every evil known to mankind has been birthed. As a result, Satan, through the fall of Adam, became the god of this present world system, ruling earth by the principles of evil, deception, and pride. The final fruits of this kingdom will be eternal judgment and separation from God in the lake of fire, which is the second death.

The blessed hope of the Christian is the return of Jesus Christ for the Church, where all born-again believers will be caught up to heaven via the rapture. But, the kingdom of darkness produces a *type* of deliverer who will usher in a limited, false peace. At the end of this short-lived peace, the world will be led into a time of trouble of such magnitude which the world has never seen, or ever will see. The one who will bring in this deceptive peace will be Satan's counterfeit deliverer, who will become the beast or the Anti-christ.

Introducing the Anti-christ

The word *Anti-christ* comes from the Greek words, *antee*, which means "opposite," and *christos*, which means "Messiah" or "Christ." Together these words form the Greek word *antechristos*, which translates into the "opponent of Christ," or the Anti-christ.

In its singular form, the word *Anti-christ* is found only four times in the New Testament, and in its plural form, it's only found once. Regardless, these words are found only in the Epistles of John. For example, in 1 John 2:18, Anti-christ is referring to the many who went out from them (the true believers). In this passage, those who went out denied that Jesus was the Christ, as well as His deity and equality with the Father. "He is antichrist, that denieth the Father and the Son" (1 John 2:22).

Since there were "*many*" (little) antichrists, their manifestation anticipates the Anti-christ who is to come (1 John 2:18).

Another use of the word *antichrist* in this Epistle is found in 1 John 4:3. Here, antichrist references the lying spirits that confess not that Jesus Christ is come in the flesh. These lying demons directly contradict the truth of the Word of God, found throughout the Scriptures, which say that Jesus was God manifested in the flesh (see John 1:1,14; 1 Tim. 3:16).

The final use of the term is in 2 John 7-10. In this passage, the *teachers* of the false doctrine, those who deny the deity of Christ, are highlighted. Of them it is said that they are deceivers; they are an antichrist.

The uses of the term in its various forms, whether it be the false teachers, individuals, or the lying spirits, are a foreshadowing of an actual person, the epitome and personification of the term. As John says, those spirits are already at work in the land and have been for a long time.

It should be noted that the person, or the human ruler, who will become the Anti-christ will be known to the world in two different phases, coinciding with both halves of the seventieth week of Daniel. The first phase will be three-and-one-half years in length as a political statesman, whose main platform will be as a peace advocate. His second phase as an evil tyrant will also be for a three-and-one-half-year period. Technically, he's only the beast, or Anti-christ, the last half of the seventieth week. In this latter half, the Bible uses different names for him, including the little horn (Dan. 7:8, 11), the beast (Rev. 13:1-8), and the son of perdition (2 Thess. 2:3-4); all of these are equivalent to the term Anti-christ. This Anti-christ will be the ruler of the earth's last great and evil Gentile world power. He will walk into the reconstructed Jewish temple and, from the throne of God, declare himself as God, demanding to be worshiped as God, under the threat of penalty of death. Such will be his strategy in the second phase, but before we go any further concerning the beast and the last half of his career, let's examine the first half.

The Rider on the White Horse

In Revelation 6, John describes four horsemen. These riders are known as the four horsemen of the apocalypse. The first one was on a white horse. Beginning at verse 2, John says, "Behold a white horse: and he that sat on him had a bow [no arrows] and a crown was given unto him and he went forth conquering and to conquer."

Here the person seen symbolically riding the white horse is the same person who will become the beast, right in the middle of the seventieth week. He will come onto the political scene as a knight in shining armor and make a covenant of peace between Israel and the surrounding nations (Dan. 9:27).

Although in his "white horse" phase he technically is not the Anti-christ or the beast yet, this person begins an evil conquest for peace, which will be his political theme for three-and-one-half years. After the three-and-one-half years of this peaceful masquerade, he will experience a sudden change of character and become the beast, or the Anti-christ. This man of sin will be followed by the rider of the red horse, who takes away the peace from the earth (Rev. 6:4).

Earlier, I discussed Daniel's seventieth week, found in Daniel, chapter 9. From the pages of this chapter, we get a glimpse of this man of sin and his career as a political statesman in quest of peace. As I mentioned before, Daniel's seventieth week is the last remaining prophetic week (seven years) awaiting fulfillment. Beginning at verse 27, the passage says:

And he [the rider on the white horse; see Rev. 6:2]
shall confirm the covenant with many for one week
[the seventieth week] and in the midst of the week
[half way, or three-and-one-half years] he shall cause
the sacrifice and the oblation to cease, and for the
overspreading of abominations he shall make it
desolate, even until the consummation, and that
determined shall be poured upon the desolate.
(Dan. 9:27)

We already know that the seventieth week will be one
prophetic time period divided into two halves. From this
passage we learn that the first half will begin with the
signing of a seven-year covenant with many. But, in the
middle of this seven-year period, the terms of the covenant which allowed Israel to have daily sacrifices and
oblations will be terminated. The rider of the white horse
(the he) will inaugurate this covenant of peace between
Israel and all the surrounding Islamic factions, possibly
including much of the international community as well.
But, all of a sudden, his character will change drastically
halfway through the seven-year covenant. He will become
the beast (Rev. 13:1-7), also known as the Anti-christ, the
tyrannical ruler of the final Gentile kingdom represented
by the ten horns (Dan. 7:7-28).

As we continue to look at this man of sin's political
career as a promoter of peace, we get a further glimpse
of his deceptive tactics from Daniel 8. Verse 25 says,
"And through his policy also he shall cause craft to prosper in his hand; and he shall magnify himself in his heart
and by peace he shall destroy many, he shall also stand up
against the Prince of princes [at Armageddon] but he
shall be broken without hand."

This amazing prophecy recounts the first half of the
seventieth week where this man of sin employs his cun-
ning and deceptive agenda for peace. The latter half of
this prophecy then looks ahead to his destruction at the
battle of Armageddon, the great battle that will take place
in the plain of Megiddo in Israel. Other scriptural evi-

dence of his deceptive peace is found in Daniel 11. Although many refer to the following scripture as having been fulfilled by Antiochus Epipanes, King of Syria, I believe that it is also prophetic.

> And in his estate shall stand up a vile person, to whom they shall not give the honour of the kingdom: but he shall come in peaceably, and obtain the kingdom by flatteries. (Dan. 11:21)

According to this passage, this man of sin shall enter without formidable opposition and obtain the kingdom by using great oratorical skill and savvy. Again, his role using peaceful deception is echoed in verse 24.

Can you imagine, as I type the pages of this book, the United States is currently applauding the peace treaty being worked out by Israel and the PLO. In stark reality, however, this treaty is just keeping the seat warm for the man of sin to occupy heralding the peace that has eluded the world ever since Israel returned to the region.

Israel, the Land of Peace

The prophecies of Ezekiel reveal more about the nature of peace introduced by the man of sin in Ezekiel 38:8; the prophet gives us a very interesting perspective of this war-torn region.

> After many days thou shall be visited: in the latter years [the end times], thou shalt come into the land that is bought back from the sword, and is gathered out of many people against the mountains of Israel, which have been always waste: but it is brought forth out of the nations, *and they shall dwell safely all of them.* (Ezek. 38:8) (emphasis mine)

This is absolutely amazing. This prophecy could not have been fulfilled until 14 May 1948, when Israel was re-established as a nation. Just as Ezekiel prophesied, in the latter years, Jews from all over the world migrated back to the land of Israel. Yet, since Israel's re-establishment, the Jews have lived in a constant state of alert and readi-

ness for war. The continuing threat of hostile attacks by
Islamic opposition forces demands that Israel be prepared
to defend her people and land. However, in the focus of
this passage, Israel's peace and safety is in view. Let's take
a look at verse 11, which says:

> And thou shalt say, I will go up to the land of
> unwalled villages; I will go to them that are at rest,
> that dwell safely, all of them dwelling without walls
> and having neither bars nor gates. (Ezek. 38:11)

Under the current hostile situations in which Israel
finds herself, it is highly unlikely that she will let down
her guards. However, the upcoming peace covenant "with
many" which Daniel references in Daniel 9:27 will allow
Israel to live at peace in the land. And, not only will Israel
and the Islamic peoples of the region be living in peace,
but Israel will be allowed to return to their system of
animal sacrifice. Sacrifice and daily oblations will be one
of the many terms of the peace treaty worked out by the
man of sin.

Before Israel can return to offering up animal sacrifices and daily oblations, she will have to rebuild the
temple. According to many sources, there is a movement
in Israel which is currently making plans to do just that.
This movement is also accompanied by the training of the
priests who will offer up the sacrifices.

It is sad irony that the Jews rejected their Messiah, yet
prepare to receive the man of sin, as prophesied by the
Lord Himself in John 5:43: "I am come in my Father's
name and ye receive me not: if another shall come in his
own name, him ye will receive." The Jews receive the man
of sin as their deliverer because of the peace that he will
bring to the region. This is why we see the false deliverer
(Rev. 6) riding in on the white horse. He will mediate this
covenant and guarantee Israel's peace and safety, and in
that part of the world, all will appear well.

Then, exactly three-and-one-half years into the covenant, this advocate of peace will affect a drastic change in

personality. He will, in this new persona, lead the world into the worst period of history ever recorded on planet earth, known as the Great Tribulation. During the three-and-one-half-year period, prior to the middle of the seventieth week, many will be basking in the sun of peace brought forth by the man of sin. But, peace shall suddenly flee from them. The Apostle Paul records in 1 Thessalonians 5:3: "For when they shall say peace and safety, then sudden destruction cometh upon them as travail upon a woman with child; and they shall not escape."

Three
❧ ❧ ❧ ❦

Who Is the Beast?

In chapter 2, I covered the first-phase characteristics of the man who will become the beast. As I pointed out, this person's two personalities will coincide with the two halves of the seventieth week of Daniel. The first half of the seventieth week, he will be a statesman who will bring peace to the Middle East via a seven-year covenant with many. During the second half, he will be the beast, or the Anti-christ. Both halves of this prophetic week will last three-and-one-half years.

In a careful study, one finds that there are three different aspects of the beast: (1) the kingdom of the beast, (2) the human monarch himself, and (3) the demon in the bottomless pit. A clear understanding of this tripartite identity is absolutely necessary if one is to understand the Scriptures which pertain to him. The relationship between the parts is vitally important, especially in light of understanding 2 Thessalonians, chapter 2.

In the book of the Revelation, there are two Greek words which translate into "beast" in English. One word is *dzo-on*, which is used in reference to the four angelic creatures found in Revelation 4, meaning "a living thing." The other Greek is *thay-ree-on*, which refers to a wild, venomous animal. By implication, *thay-ree-on* was used, for example, when a dangerous animal was to be hunted down and destroyed. It is the latter term for beast that appropriately applies to the dictator of the world's final Gentile kingdom, the Anti-christ.

The Kingdom of the Beast

In Revelation 13, John gives us a symbolic description of the beast.

> And I stood upon the sand of the sea, and saw a beast rise up out of the sea, having seven heads and ten horns, and upon his horns ten crowns, and upon his heads the name of blasphemy. And the beast which I saw was like unto a leopard, and his feet were as the feet of a bear, and his mouth as the mouth of a lion: and the dragon gave him his power, and his seat, and great authority. (Rev. 13:1-2)

In chapter 1, I covered Daniel 7, which concerned Daniel's dream of the four beasts. Those four beasts represented four great Gentile empires: Babylon the lion, Medo-Persia the bear, Greece the leopard, and a fourth beast, Rome. From the Revelation account, we see that the "beast" will be comprised of elements of the historical empires seen in Daniel. However, this beast will be different from the other beast before him in that he will be exceedingly dreadful, having ten horns (Dan. 7:7).

These ten horns, mentioned in both Daniel and Revelation, are said to have on them ten crowns. This represents a ten-nation confederacy, consisting of countries that have roots in the ancient Roman empire (Dan. 7:23-24). Many believe that these ten nations will come out of the European Economic Common Market. So, from both the historic and the futuristic viewpoints, we detect the structure and the elements in which the kingdom of the beast shall stand upon.

The Human Monarch

The next aspect of the beast that I would like to examine is the person who will become the beast, or the Anti-christ. Again, we must return to the book of Daniel to get a look at this character. In Daniel 7, there are some key verses that describe the beast's actions. Let's begin at verse 8:

> I considered the horns [ten horns] and, behold, there came up among them another little horn, before whom there were three of the first horns plucked up by the roots: and behold, in this horn were eyes like the eyes of a man, and a mouth speaking great things.

In this passage, the beast is identified as being a man that will pluck up three of the other horns by the roots and speak great things. Perhaps the uprooting of the three is in reference to some kind of political coup. Let's jump to verse 25:

> And he shall speak great words against the most High, and shall wear out the saints of the most High, and think to change times and laws: and they shall be given into his hand until a time and times and the dividing of time.

Here, some more important information about this man is provided. First of all, he will speak blasphemy against God and make war with God's saints, killing many of them. He will also alter established times and laws, which would probably include removing the daily sacrifice system and any laws concerning the worship of any god other than himself (Dan. 9:27; 2 Thess. 2:4). And, finally we find out exactly how long he will have to work out his evil agenda. The phrase that is used to tell us this is: "time, times, and the dividing of time." The word translated as *time* in this verse comes from the Hebrew word *id-dawn*, which means "one year." The word *times* means "two years"; so the "dividing of time" is one-half year, totaling three-and-one-half years. The beast has this much time to rule as the beast, coinciding with the last half of the seventieth week, exactly as we are told in Revelation 13:5, concerning his time of rule, forty-two months (i.e., forty-two thirty-day months). Why is three-and-one-half years so significant? Because three-and-one-half years is exactly half of the seven-year period, the total time frame of the seventieth week of Daniel.

The beast will begin his reign as earth's final Gentile tyrant and directly under satanic control (not possession). He will then initiate the abomination of desolation, walk into the Most Holy Place of the Jewish temple, and declare himself God, demanding appropriate worship (see Dan. 7:8, 25; 9:27; Rev. 3:1-8; 2 Thess. 2:4).

It is important to remember that Revelation 6 depicts him as the rider on the white horse during the first half of the seventieth week. His political theme will be peace. The important question at this point is: What will make him change? What will make him forsake the covenant of peace which he instituted just three-and-one-half years prior? Why will he change into the world's worst tyrant? The answer can be found in the analysis of the last aspect of the beast, the demon out of the bottomless pit!

The Demon Out of the Bottomless Pit

Although many authoritative theologians have written prolifically on this topic, I have yet to read a single author who probes the demonic aspect of the beast. Many say that it is Satan himself who possesses the beast, but I will show you that this is not so. In this section, I will demonstrate to you that a demon, who is a resident of the bottomless pit, will in fact possess the man of sin, transforming him into the son of perdition, also known as the beast (2 Thess. 2:3-4).

In Revelation 17, the Apostle John is having a conversation with an angel who begins to explain the symbology of the beast. In verse 7, the angel says, "I will tell you the mystery [the secret] of the woman, and of the beast that carrieth her, which hath the seven heads and ten horns" (See also Rev. 13:1-8.). Then in verse 8, he begins to tell John the "hidden truth" behind the beast, who John saw rise out of the sea in chapter 13. It is vitally important that this analysis is closely followed here in order to understand the real truth about the beast. The angel says:

> The beast that thou sawest, was and is not; and shall ascend out of the bottomless pit [the Abyss], and go into perdition: And they that dwell on the earth shall wonder, whose names were not written in the book of life from the foundation of the world, when they behold the beast that was, and is not, and yet is. (Rev. 17:8)

In this Scripture, we get a very interesting view of the beast. Without a doubt, the beast shall come out of the bottomless pit. From this passage, it is also clear that the beast is a demon bearing the exact same symbols as his human counterpart does (Rev. 13:1-3). Since this aspect of the beast ascends from the bottomless pit, that means he's a resident of the pit.

Now some interpret this passage as referring to the reconstructed Roman Empire under the influence of Satan's power. I understand why that interpretation is taken that way. The symbols (seven heads and ten horns) are geo-political in other passages. But, in this passage, governmental structure isn't the theme. The object under analysis here is the demon who will possess the Antichrist. Governments don't live in the bottomless pit; demons do.

The term "bottomless pit" comes from the Greek word *ab-us-sos*, which is translated "abyss" or "bottomless pit." Whenever this term is used in Revelation, it's always in reference to demons. The bottomless pit is a fiery place of torment where demonic spirits are kept in detention. For example, Jude alludes to this demonic detention by telling us that these fallen angels are reserved unto judgment under darkness in "everlasting chains" (Jude 6). From the Abyss, demons are released for service in the satanic sphere here on earth and in the lower heavenly realms for specific amounts of time (more on this later).

Upon further examination of verse 8, this demon's times of involvement in the earthly realm are revealed. The angel says that the beast "was, and is not and shall ascend out of the bottomless pit." Then he goes on to say, "And they that dwell on the earth . . . shall wonder, when they behold the beast that was, is not, and yet is." At first this passage may seem confusing, but it makes a lot of sense when understood properly. The phrase "was, is not, and shall" are three tenses of time (past, present, and future) relative to John's day. These tenses of time apply to the demon. For example, the demon was, i.e., prior to John's days, and is not, i.e., during John's days, but shall ascend out of the pit, i.e., beyond or in the future of John's days. From the demon's perspective, he *was* loose, or out of the bottomless pit prior to John's days; he *is not* while detained in the bottomless pit during John's days; and *shall ascend out,* or let loose again, in the future of John's days.

In verse 10, more symbols are used to describe this demon: "There are seven kings: five are fallen, and one is, and the other is not yet come; and when he cometh, he must continue a short space."

In this passage the angel tells John that there shall be seven kings or kingdoms to rise on the world scene. Five of these kingdoms were already fallen; one of them was, and the other hadn't yet come during John's time. Easily identified is the kingdom that was in power during John's day—Rome; Domitian, Emperor of Rome, was the one who banished John to the island of Patmos, where he wrote the book of the Revelation. Rome was the kingdom that "is."

To get a good understanding of the five kingdoms that are fallen, we must understand that Satan has had a specific network of powerful nations. Over the centuries, the devil has used major Gentile kingdoms to pursue and persecute the nation of Israel. Although it would be God's divine providence to determine the who, when, and where of Israel's persecution for her various national sins, God would operate through Gentile nations controlled by Satan to accomplish His will.

The Great Symbols

In Revelation 12, the nation of Israel is symbolized as a woman wearing a crown of twelve stars, representing the twelve tribes of Israel. The woman then brought forth a man child (Jesus Christ) who was caught up to His Father's throne. The woman was persecuted by the dragon (Satan), but she had a place prepared in the wilderness where she would be nourished for a time, times, and half a time (three-and-one-half years). This symbol of Israel is historic as well as prophetic, speaking of her history prior to Christ, His birth and Resurrection, as well as her future during the second half of the seventieth week (Rev. 12:1-2, 5-6, 13-17).

Another symbol with significance is the great red dragon with seven heads and ten horns. It is said of this dragon that his tail drew a third of the stars of heaven and cast them to the earth. The dragon then stood by and waited for the woman to bring forth her child, so that he could devour him as soon as he was born. This dragon lost an angelic war in heaven and was cast out. He was very angry and went about to persecute the remnant of the seed of the woman.

Just as Israel's kingdom is depicted symbolically, so is Satan's kingdom shown symbolically. And similarly, just as Israel's symbol was historic, geo-political, and futuristic, so is Satan's symbol. This is the most well known illustration of Satan's heavenly rebellion, because it says that he drew a third of the stars (or angels) of heaven. In the symbol, the devil waited for the birth of Christ to devour him as soon as he was born (Remember King Herod's edict?). Then the symbol reveals the future where the dragon (Satan) pursues Israel during the last half of the seventieth week. This red dragon has seven heads and ten horns.

It is clear here that this symbol is a reference to Satan's historic and future kingdom, stemming from his rebellion in heaven all the way into the future during the seventieth week. From this passage many have supposed that Satan himself will possess the beast. Because Satan is identified with the seven heads and ten horns, which are also the symbols used to describe the beast in Revelation 13, many believe that they are one and the same. But, this is an error; this symbol is wholly historical, geo-political, and futuristic, revealing to us the network of satanic nations used to persecute Israel over the centuries. It has certainly been Satan's evil influence upon these kingdoms that has allowed them to be so successful in carrying out his wicked schemes for Israel.

With this in mind, all one would have to do is read the Old and New Testaments to find out who six of the seven heads are, five of which having already fallen by John's writing (Rev. 17:10). Five great nations persecuted and ruled over Israel prior to the Romans: Egypt, Babylon, Medo-Persia, Greece, and Syria. Rome, number six, was in power during John's day, and the final, seventh kingdom had not yet come.

It is my belief that the seventh kingdom was Germany under the dictatorship of Adolf Hitler. Hitler's great hatred for the Jews was renowned; we are all quite aware that his attentions were to completely exterminate the whole race. In Hitler's strategy, his own genetically engineered Aryan race would rule the world with him; none other could be worthy of the role. As history records, Hitler's evil plans failed, and Germany was conquered, their leader opting for cowardice and suicide. Then, following the murder of millions of Jews, God re-established the nation of Israel. It was as though God was mocking Hitler's impotent attempt to destroy His chosen people.

In comparison to the other six empires, Germany's reign was for a very short time.

The Eighth King

Let's return to Revelation 17:11.

> And the beast that was, and is not even he is the eighth, and is of the seven and goeth into perdition.

From this passage we see that the beast that "was" and "is not" is of the seven. This means that the beast of the bottomless pit was a power player in one of those kingdoms. This is why "he was," prior to John's days, but during John's days, he was banished and locked in the bottomless pit, where he was rendered completely inactive. This is why the angel told John that the beast *is not*, but he *yet is* and *shall ascend out of the bottomless pit* in the future.

When this demon is released out of the bottomless pit, he will actually become the eighth head (Rev. 17:11) in his encore appearance on the world scene. Once this ancient demon is released to rule through his human counterpart, the son of perdition, he will get another chance to persecute the nation of Israel.

The Beast, Not Satan

Could it be Satan who possesses the beast, as many claim? Many who say yes to this question refer to Revelation 12 as a proof text. But, what one must keep in mind is that it is historical, geo-political and futuristic. Because it is a picture of Satan's network of nations as it has manifested itself over the centuries, he's obviously identified as the chief principality and power behind the persecution of Israel; this is also seen in Revelation 13. The beast's kingdom contains elements of past, satanically inspired nations such as Persia, Greece, and Babylon. In one way or another, these are all satanically linked, but this in no way implies that Satan himself is going to possess the beast.

A careful review of the Scriptures shows that it is not Satan who will possess the beast. First of all, the beast ascends from the bottomless pit (Rev. 17:8). There are absolutely no Scriptures which say Satan is in the bottomless pit. The pit is a prison for demons, and they don't just go in and out as they please. Satan will be thrown into the bottomless pit when the Lord returns, but it will only be for a thousand years (Rev. 20:1-3).

This account is the only actual reference to Satan ever being in the bottomless pit, and he certainly wasn't in the pit in John's day. The *beast* was in the bottomless pit at that time which is why Revelation 17:8 says he "is not . . . yet is." According to John, Satan had a seat somewhere in or around Pergamos (Rev. 2:13).

Jesus Himself referred to Satan as the prince of this world (specifically, this world system, in John 16:11). Paul refers to Satan as "the god of this world" and the "prince and power of the air" (2 Cor. 4:4, Eph. 2:2). Seen before the throne of God in the testing of Job (1:6), he is thus the accuser of the brethren before God (Rev. 12:10). He also contended with the archangel Michael over the body of Moses (Jude 9). He was free to tempt Jesus in the wilderness (Matt. 4:1-11). It is clear that Satan is not locked up in the bottomless pit.

Out of all of these Scriptures the clearest, showing an undeniable difference between Satan and the demon who possesses the Anti-christ, is found in Revelation 19. In verse 20, we are told that the beast and the false prophet were both cast alive into the lake of fire. However, in Revelation 20:1-3, Satan was cast into the bottomless pit for a thousand years. After the thousand years are over, and Satan leads the world in one last rebellion, he will be thrown into the lake of fire, where the beast and the false prophet already *are* (Rev. 20:7-10).

So, as you can see from all these passages of Scripture, the beast and Satan are not the same evil spirit, although the beast's human counterpart, through whom the beast will rule, gets his seat and great authority from Satan. There is no biblical evidence that Satan himself possesses the Anti-christ.

The Beast with the Deadly Wound

Another misleading area of popular interpretation is John's testimony of one of the seven heads wounded to death (Rev. 13:3). Many have interpreted this passage to mean that the Anti-christ will be shot in the head and then be miraculously restored to life. Although at first this may seem plausible, this interpretation fails to consider the information the angel gives to John in Revelation 17. When the beast is said to be "is not," he is locked in the bottomless pit and rendered totally inactive as though he were dead, but, as we know, he "yet is" (Rev. 17:8).

I believe Revelation 13:3 refers to the demon's *return* to the world scene. My reasoning stems from what the passage says in Revelation 17:8; let's take a look at it.

> And they that dwell on the earth shall wonder . . . when they behold the beast that was, and is not, and yet is. (Rev. 13:3; 17:8)

The world wondered after the beast, when his deadly wound was healed. Putting the information together from both passages, one can understand exactly what the angel was telling John about this demon: The world shall wonder when they behold the beast upon his release! When this demon is freed from the bottomless pit (for he "shall" ascend out of the bottomless pit), he will no longer be "is not"! What causes the world to wonder about the beast is the sight of this demon manifested in his *human* counterpart. This is what the healing of the deadly wound really references. The demon has been kept inside the bottomless pit for a long time now, but he shall ascend out of the bottomless pit, in the middle of the seventieth week, and rule through this human counterpart, the son of perdition (2 Thess. 2:3-4).

Four

꙰꙰ ꙰꙰

The Abomination of Desolation

As I have discussed earlier, the man of sin begins the seventieth week as a peace advocate and establishes a covenant of peace with many for a seven-year period. The inauguration of this covenant will obviously be a major fulfillment of events that must come to pass according to God's prophetic calendar. However, there will be another major event that will follow 1,290 days later.

In Mark 13:14, Jesus refers to a prophetic event called the abomination of desolation. Let's take a look at this passage:

> But when ye shall see the abomination of desola-
> tion, spoken of by Daniel the prophet, standing
> where it ought not, (let him that readeth under-

stand,) then let them that are in Judæa flee to the mountains.

What is this abomination of desolation? According to the *American Heritage Dictionary*, the word *abomination* means: "an abhorrence for something or someone, loathsome or something that elicits great dislike." In the Hebrew tongue, the word that applies to this passage is the word *shik-koots*, which means "disgusting," i.e., something that's filthy, especially an idol or some other detestable thing.

Because the Lord Himself referred to Daniel the prophet in reference to the abomination of desolation, then that's where we must go to understand exactly what this means.

In Daniel 9, the prophet gives us insight concerning this upcoming event. Beginning at verse 27, the passage says:

> And he shall confirm the covenant with many for one week and in the midst of the week he shall cause the sacrifice and the oblation to cease, and for the overspreading of abominations he shall make it desolate, even until the consummation, and that determined shall be poured out upon the desolate.

As I stated earlier, the man of sin will establish a covenant between Jews and the Islamic factions warring against Israel. The term of this covenant will be seven years, which coincides with the seventieth week of Daniel. This treaty will also allow Israel to return to the system of animal sacrifice and daily oblations (offerings) to God. But, three-and-one-half years into this treaty, the man of sin will have a sudden change of character and will become the beast, who is also the son of perdition. He will forsake the terms of the treaty that he made with Israel and take away the right to the daily sacrifices and oblations. Soon afterwards, he shall enact the abomination of desolation, and the temple will be laid waste and ruined.

In Daniel 11, we get another view of the abomination of desolation. Beginning at verse 31, the passage says:

> And arms shall stand on his part, and they shall pollute the sanctuary of strength, and shall take away the daily sacrifice, and they shall place the abomination that maketh it desolate.

According to many expositors and historians, Daniel 11:21-35 is in reference to Antiochus Epiphanes, king of Syria, who entered the most holy place of the Jewish temple and sacrificed a sow on the altar there. He also took away the Jews' right to sacrifice, which has been guaranteed by covenant.

Whether or not this is true is not the issue. What's important is that the *beast* will place the abomination of desolation. The historic actions described here serve as a prototype of the actions of the beast in the middle of the seventieth week, which, according to verse 35, is "even to the time of the end:" because the vision is yet for an appointed time.

Contained in this passage is a very interesting piece of information, providing us some more insight into the abomination of desolation. First of all, the passage says that the abomination of desolation is to be *placed*. In Matthew 24:15 and in Mark 13:14, Jesus tells us that the abomination of desolation is seen "standing" in the Holy Place. Then in Daniel 12:11, it is said that the "abomination that maketh it desolate is *set up*" (emphasis mine).

Remember the definition of the word *abomination* (*shik-koots*), which referred to a disgusting thing, especially an idol? Well, let's look at it, and put all the references together. The abomination of desolation is an abominable "thing" that needs to be "set up" and "placed" and will be seen "standing" in the Holy Place where it ought not be. So what could this all possibly mean? To answer that question I must return to Revelation 13 to uncover the mystery of the abomination of desolation.

Introducing the False Prophet

As one reads the book of the Revelation, no study of the beast would be quite complete without examining the false prophet.

> And I beheld another beast coming up out of the earth; and he had two horns like a lamb, and spake as a dragon. And he exerciseth all the power of the first beast before him and causeth the earth and them which dwell therein to worship the first beast, whose deadly wound was healed. And he doeth great wonders so that he maketh fire come down from heaven on the earth in the sight of men, And deceiveth them that dwell on the earth by the means of those miracles which he had power to do in the sight of the beast; saying to them that dwell on the earth, that they should make an image to the beast which had the deadly wound by a sword, and did live. (Rev. 13:11-14)

Now this tyrannical clergyman will be quite impressive. As the way to get complete control over the people of the earth, Anti-christ will employ the services of the false prophet. Since the nature of man tends to be rebellious, the false prophet's "lying wonder miracles" will be enough to persuade the most staunch doubters. And, through his satanically inspired powers, he will cause the world to worship the beast. But this is not all; first he will cause the people to make an image of the beast and then bring the image to life!

Revelation 13:15 says:

> And he had power to give life unto the image of the beast, that the image of the beast should both speak, and cause that as many as would not worship the image of the beast should be killed.

Of all the diabolical and hideous abominations that the Anti-christ and false prophet perpetrate, this will be the absolute epitome of them all. The edict will also be issued that failure to worship the image of the beast will result in sure death. This will be the *abomination* that will be *placed* in the Most Holiest, rendering the area desolate and desecrated.

The abominations that the beast and the false prophet will do in God's temple by far surpass the actions that were done by Antiochus. Again, I'm not saying that the historians are wrong about the historic fulfillment of Daniel 11; I just think it would be a mistake to lock ourselves into the historic interpretation only.

The reason why I say this is because I believe that Daniel 11:31 does in fact give us a glimpse of the false prophet's role in the abomination of desolation.

> And arms shall stand on his part, and they shall pollute the sanctuary of strength, and shall take away the daily sacrifice and they shall place the abomination that maketh desolate.

Notice this passage's reference to arms standing on his side; the singular pronoun *his* is used. But, when the passage refers to the abomination of desolation, the plural pronoun *they* is used. This is because this passage prophetically anticipates the role of the false prophet in placing the abomination of desolation, to occur exactly thirty days after the beast takes away the daily sacrifice, according to Daniel 12:11:

> And from the time that the daily sacrifice shall be taken away and the abomination of desolation set up, there shall be a thousand two hundred and ninety days [1,290].

One thousand two hundred and ninety days is thirty days more than 1,260 days. The 1,260 days is the exact amount of days contained in three-and-one-half years, using thirty-day months. The use of 1,260 days can also be found in Revelation 11:3. Twelve hundred and sixty days coincides with the amount of days contained in either half of the seventieth week, which is divided into two forty-two-month segments.

As though the abomination of desolation alone won't be bad enough, the beast shall add insult to injury. According to the Apostle Paul, the beast shall declare himself as God while sitting in the temple of God. (In the next chapter, I shall cover this in great detail.) Referring again to Daniel 9:27, the passage says: "for the overspreading of abominations." Not only will the false prophet and the beast set up the beast's image in the Most Holy Place, but the beast himself shall enter it and declare himself to be God.

Five

The Revealing of the Anti-christ

The Anti-christ is also known as the son of perdition, the beast, and the little horn. Although all these names apply to the same man, the proper interpretation of key Scriptures concerning him is vitally important. Much confusion and bad doctrine has circulated throughout the Church for years concerning the revealing of Anti-christ. One of the problems seems to hinge on the proper interpretation and definition of the word *revealed*.

Whole doctrinal positions have been taught and widely accepted as the truth, even though no Scripture backs them up. Ladies and gentlemen, fellow saints and friends, the next three chapters of this book may change your life and your view on the end times.

Let's begin our study by looking at 2 Thessalonians 2:1-3. Paul says:

> Now we beseech you, brethren, by the coming of
> our Lord Jesus Christ, and by our gathering to-
> gether unto him, That ye be not soon shaken in
> mind, or be troubled, neither by spirit, nor by
> word, nor by letter as from us, as that the day of
> Christ [day of the Lord] is at hand. Let no man
> deceive you by any means: for that day shall not
> come, except there come a falling away first, and
> that man of sin be revealed, the son of perdition.

Paul addressed the saints at the church of Thessalonica
concerning the coming of our Lord and our "gathering"
(the rapture) unto him. Specifically, he urged them not to
be "soon shaken in mind, or troubled," or fearing that
the day of the Lord was upon them.

Now, earlier in the Epistle (2 Thess. 1:4-9), it is revealed that this congregation was undergoing severe per-
secutions and trials. Incidentally, someone had written
them a letter saying that the day of the Lord was already
occurring. The unfortunate thing about this was that it
appeared that Paul's name was forged as the sender of
the letter. Can you imagine what was going through the
minds of this congregation? Without a doubt, the fact
that they thought they were in the day of the Lord would
create some very interesting problems.

Over the years many have tried to get into the mind
of this ancient church. In the process of doing so, numerous interesting theories concerning their situation have
arisen. One of those theories is: Since the Thessalonians
had received this forged letter and accepted it as the
truth, it caused them to be "shaken in mind and troubled."
They became nonproductive, believing that the day of the
Lord was upon them, and sadness overtook in many because they would have to relinquish their livelihoods and
careers. In my opinion, the above scenario misses the
mark considerably.

According to Paul's First Epistle to the Thessalonians,
he had previously instructed this congregation concerning the day of the Lord and told them, "for God hath not

appointed us to wrath" (1 Thess. 5:9). We know that the wrath of which Paul was speaking was the day of the Lord (cf. v. 2). Paul had also covered the rapture of the Church to reassure those who had already lost loved ones. Paul told them that he had received an instruction from the Lord that the dead "in Christ" would be the first ones to rise at the Lord's return; then the living would be caught up and they would all meet the Lord in the clouds together and forever be with Him.

Even though the Thessalonians had been instructed in this matter, they received the forged "day of the Lord" letter and became (understandably) anxious. The Church was supposed to be removed prior to the day of the Lord, but according to the bogus letter, claiming the authority of Paul, the day of the Lord was now evidently upon them. This left the Thessalonians with some critical options: Either Paul was now recanting what he had taught them earlier about the timing of the rapture, or this admonition meant that the resurrection (i.e., the rapture) had occurred already.

Keep in mind, the Thessalonians believed the bogus letter was authentic. Therefore, in either case, this news had adverse effects on their faith. This is why, when Paul writes the second Epistle, he tells them to not be anxious concerning the supposedly imminent gathering to Christ and the day of the Lord. He then strongly emphasizes his instruction, as if he were saying: "No matter who it's from don't believe it." Even if by a spirit, a word, or a letter from Paul or his disciples, *do not believe* that the day of the Lord is at hand.

Consider the dilemma the Thessalonians were in, faced with thinking that they had missed the resurrection or coming to the stark reality that what they had been taught was obviously the wrong thing. Either one of these cases would be a critical issue to any Christian of any era, particularly in the face of harsh persecution.

The rapture of the Church is our "Blessed Hope," and it is the reason why we are able to endure the tribulation

of this world. The Apostle Paul assures us that if there is
no resurrection, our faith is in vain. And, if our hope is in
this life only, then we are of all men most miserable (1 Cor.
15:16-19). The wretched Thessalonians had the hope of
the resurrection snatched from them, and it shook their
faith!

This false doctrine was not unusual in those days. In
2 Timothy 2:18, Paul warns Timothy about the similar
doctrine of Hymenæus and Philetus:

> Who concerning the truth have erred, saying that
> the resurrection is past already; overthrowing the
> faith of some.

Paul grieved that this teaching was as destructive as
cancer or gangrene. Just as the Scriptures say, "There is
no new thing under the sun" (Eccles. 1:9), this scenario
will happen again.

That Day Shall Not Come

To ease the Thessalonians' anxiety, Paul told them
that two things must occur before the day of the Lord.

> Let no man deceive you by any means: for that
> day shall not come, except there come a falling
> away first, and the man of sin be revealed, the son
> of perdition. (2 Thess. 2:3)

Paul says that there must first come a falling away.
The word *falling* comes from the Greek word *apostasia*,
which means "to defect from the truth." Paul doesn't
elaborate on the manner of apostasy here but proceeds to
the next thing that must occur prior to the day of the
Lord: the "man of sin" must be revealed as the son of
perdition. In this passage there is one word that seems to
cause a major doctrinal problem for many who attempt
to interpret its meaning. This word is *revealed*.

The word *revealed* is translated from the Greek word
apokalupto, which means to "uncover" or to "disclose." As
a transitive verb, it requires that someone or something
be uncovered or disclosed. It does not mean to "see

initially," nor does it mean "first appearance" or "the first time on a scene, or on a particular setting." There is a word that is translated "revealed" in English, and it's a similar word to *apokalupto*. For example, in 2 Thessalonians 1:7, "When the Lord Jesus shall be revealed from heaven with his mighty angels . . . ," the Greek word that is used here is *apokalupsis*, which means "a manifestation, a coming or an appearing."

The word *apokalupto* is a compound word that comes from the Greek roots *apo* (reversal, or departure) and *kalupto* (to cover something up, or to hide something or someone). *Apokalupto* means the uncovering of something that's been hidden. "Revealed" is in relationship to the man of sin being "uncovered" as the son of perdition—not "initially" identified.

In chapter 2, I recounted how the man of sin will usher in a short-lived time of peace by way of a peace treaty, inaugurated in the beginning of the seventieth week of Daniel (Dan. 9:27). Israel and the world's nations will willingly receive this man because he will have the solution for a peace for which the world has been starving. So Satan takes advantage of this situation and gives the world exactly what they "think" they want.

This deceptive peace on the international political scene will be the cover-up that will buy him worldwide acceptance. Remember the rider of the white horse in Revelation 6? He will come in with peace and make the covenant with many. Israel will become the land of unwalled villages and will return to animal sacrifices and the offering up of daily oblations (Rev. 6:2; Dan. 9:27; Ezek. 38:8, 11). This will be the greatest masquerade and satanic cover-up of all time! And, the people of the earth are going to buy it.

Now, the horrible thing about this passage is if the *wrong* Greek word, *apokalupsis*, is used or the interpretation for the word *revealed* is determined to be "identify initially," "the first appearance," or his "coming," one might be led into thinking that this revealing was in reference to the beginning of the seventieth week, where the man of sin makes an initial appearance. However, this is a *major* interpretive error.

Again, the proper Greek word in this text is *apokalupto.* When the man of sin comes on the scene, the peace he brings in will be Satan's cloak under which the devil's intentions for the world's course will be hidden. After three-and-one-half years, Satan's real agenda for this person (the man of sin) will be uncovered. He will then transform from his "man of sin," white horse symbology, into the son of perdition or the beast, who has the seven heads and ten horns symbology.

After the uncovering, or revealing, occurs, he will renege on the terms of the treaty he made with Israel by taking away the daily sacrifice and oblation. Then some thirty days later, he will place the abomination that will desecrate the Jewish temple. Paul describes this man's new character and what it is he will do when he's uncovered. In 2 Thessalonians 2:4, Paul says:

> Who opposeth and exalteth himself above all that is called God, or that is worshiped; so that he as God sitteth in the temple of God, shewing himself that he is God.

Remember that the definition of the Anti-christ means an "opponent of Christ." This is exactly how Daniel and John tell us Anti-christ begins his forty-two-month reign: by opposing God (Dan. 7:25; Rev. 13:5). What Paul is depicting here is an account of the abomination of desolation, just one of many the son of perdition (the beast) will commit, along with the false prophet, in the Holy Place of the rebuilt temple (cf Rev. 13, Dan. 9:27). This passage doesn't list any of this man's characteristics associated with the first half of the seventieth week. That's particularly strange—if what Paul was speaking of was an *apokalupsis* (appearance or coming) of the "man of sin" at the beginning of the seventieth week.

The man of sin will be *identified* at the beginning of

the seventieth week, but the son of perdition cannot be *uncovered* until the middle of the week. The *uncovering* of the son of perdition is the focus of this and the following passage (vv. 3 and 4). I believe Paul wrote it this way so that we wouldn't become confused about his beginning and the middle of the week characteristics.

The fourth verse clearly describes the abomination of desolation, which would obviously have to occur before: "That which is determined [Wrath] is poured out on the desolator [the beast]" (Dan 9:27). Absolutely none of the actions Paul describes in verse 4 can be attributed to the man of sin's political agenda of peace during the first half of the seventieth week. Does the man of sin come on the scene calling himself God? No. Does the man of sin sit on the throne of God at the beginning of the seventieth week? No. Does the man of sin come on the scene blaspheming God? Not according to the Scriptures. Does the man of sin place the abomination of desolation in the beginning of the week? Does the son of perdition have all seven years of the seventieth week to rule as the beast? No, only forty-two months.

Paul explains to the Thessalonians in his first Epistle: "For when they shall say, Peace and safety; then sudden destruction cometh upon them . . ." (1 Thess. 5:3).

The interpretation of the word *revealed* has a drastic effect on full interpretation of this passage. Unfortunately, this isn't the only word in 2 Thessalonians 2 to be misinterpreted by centuries of theologians. *He* and *what* and their misinterpretations will be dealt with in the next two chapters. The doctrines which have evolved from misinterpretations of these two words are absolutely amazing.

The "What" That Now Withholds

What one has been taught about the rapture, or how one has been taught, has an impact on which position they adopt themselves—for many it's the one that sounds the best. The pre-trib doctrine teaches that the Church won't be here during any part of the seventieth week of Daniel, meaning Christians won't have to suffer the devil's wrath. But this is wrong! There isn't *one* Scripture guaranteeing that Christians will be delivered from either the wrath of the devil or his persecution.

As we continue our study in the book of 2 Thessalonians 2, I will be unraveling some more truths that are contained in this chapter and hopefully clear up some of the above misunderstandings. As I stated in chapter 5, there are three key words in this passage that are crucial to interpreting the chapter properly. The first one is *revealed*, covered in chapter 5. The other two are *what* and *he*, found in verses 6 and 7, respectively.

To the casual observer, these may appear to be very insignificant words, but they have been the focal point of a lot of exegesis. Because of what they represent, it is vital to know exactly to whom or what they refer. Whole doctrines have been spawned from their misinterpretations; their wrong understanding has a devastating potential to many Christians.

Let's take a look at what Paul tells this congregation in verses 5–7:

> Remember ye not, that, when I was yet with you,
> I told you these things? And now ye know what
> withholdeth that he might be revealed in his time.
> For the mystery of iniquity doeth already work:
> only he who now letteth will let until he be taken
> out of the way.

It is apparent that Paul had already instructed this congregation about the identity of that which restrains the revealing of the son of perdition. The identity of the "*what* that now withholds" and the "*he* who now letteth" has been the object of much debate. Theologians have considered this subject for a long time, but particularly in the last hundred years.

The logical question concerning this restraining force is: Who or what is capable of restraining the revealing of the beast? One of the theories is that it is a form of human government. Another one is that Satan himself is the restrainer. I agree with many of my colleagues that neither one of these interpretations hold water.

The final and seemingly the most tenable of the current theories is that the Holy Spirit Himself restrains the revealing of the son of perdition. Although this interpretation sounds the best, compared to the others, this too is wrong. This very interpretation is why I'm writing this book. More than any other Scripture in the Bible, 2 Thessalonians 2 is the flagship of the pre-trib doctrine, and it is anchored by the identification of the *what* and the *he*.

Because of the interpretation of the *he* and the *what* as being the Holy Spirit in the Church, two doctrines have developed: (1) The Holy Spirit will be taken from the earth during the seventieth week; and (2) The Holy Spirit has "the restraining ministry."

In the next two chapters, I will challenge these doctrines with direct scriptural proofs that will unequivocally show a different interpretation. As one Bible reference commentary puts it, concerning the identity of the *he* and the *what*: The restrainer is a person ("he"), and since a mystery always implies a supernatural element, this "Person" can be none other than the Holy Spirit in the Church, to be taken out of the way.

That interpretation of the passage is probably one of the most, if not *the* most, prevalent interpretations in Christian eschatological circles today. Pre-tribers say the Holy Spirit ("he") in the Church will be taken out of the way prior to the revealing of the son of perdition. This meaning is coupled with the earlier reading of the *revealing* of the son of perdition as occurring when the man of sin is seen initially at the beginning of the seventieth week of Daniel.

To continue with the pre-triber logic, the Holy Spirit resides in the Church and the Holy Spirit must be taken out of the way before the revealing of the son of perdition (the beast). In conjunction with that, since the Antichrist will be revealed when he inaugurates the peace covenant at the beginning of the seventieth week, the Holy Spirit and the Church will be gone prior to the seventieth week. Before I refute this teaching I want to review all we have learned about the beast.

Paul opens up 2 Thessalonians 2, speaking of two events: The gathering of the saints unto the Lord when He returns for the Church (v. 1), and the day of the Lord (v. 2). Paul makes it clear earlier that the rapture would occur prior to the day of the Lord (1 Thess. 5:2,9); he then tells them that two things must occur prior to the day of the Lord (2 Thess. 2:3). These two things are the falling away and the revealing of the son of perdition. Paul doesn't elaborate on the falling away in this passage but goes on to explain the revealing of the son of perdition (2 Thess. 2:3-4). Paul then informs them that the son of perdition can't be revealed until the restrainer is first removed (2 Thess. 2:7). Paul identifies the restrainer as a *what* that was withholding, or hindering, and a *he* who restrains.

At this point, I must say that Paul himself does not identify the *he* or the *what* as being the Holy Spirit. He had already told them who was doing the restraining (verse 5), but we don't have an account of exactly what he told them, nor when he told them. He just says, "Remember when I was with you before, I told you these things." Since we don't know what Paul told them, I won't speculate, but let's look at what the rest of the Bible says about it.

In chapter 3, I covered the tri-part personality of the beast, representing three things: (1) the kingdom of the beast, (2) the human monarch or dictator himself, and (3) the demon that shall ascend out of the bottomless pit. Without understanding this, one cannot interpret 2 Thessalonians properly, especially the third aspect of the beast, the demon. This is the aspect of the beast that has been overlooked for years. Because many have just assumed that it is Satan who possesses the beast, Revelation 17:8 has been ignored, or misinterpreted.

The Bottomless Pit

In Revelation 17:8, we find the angelic interpretation of the mystery of the "beast" which John first sees in chapter 13. The angel clearly tells John that the beast that thou sawest, having seven heads and ten horns, shall ascend out of the *bottomless pit*.

As I stated before, the bottomless pit is a fiery place of detention for demonic spirits. In Revelation, every mention of the bottomless pit is in connection with demons. In chapter 9, locust-like demons are depicted proceeding out of the bottomless pit. The bottomless pit also has an angel over it, named Abaddon, in the Hebrew tongue, or Apollyon, in the Greek. I believe the bottomless pit is located somewhere on the earth, because when the pit was opened to release the demon locusts out of it, the sun was darkened as a result of the rising smoke that billowed out of it.

In Revelation 20, we see that Satan will be thrown into the bottomless pit and locked up in it for one thousand years. This tells us something about the integrity of this pit. If the chief of all evil principality and power, Satan himself, can be locked in the bottomless pit without the possibility of escape, then so can any other demon!

When I did the study on who is the beast, we covered the actions of the beast. We know that during the first half of the seventieth week, the man of sin will be a peace advocate who brings in the peace by a seven-year covenant. We also know that Israel will become a land of unwalled villages and return to its system of animal sacrifice (Dan. 9:27; Ezek. 38:8, 11). This man of sin, in his peaceful masquerade, is symbolized by the white horse in Revelation 6:2.

However, in the middle of the seventieth week, the man of sin's character will change for the worst. He will renege on the peace treaty with Israel. He will also take away their daily sacrifices. He will place the abomination that desecrates the Most Holy Place of the Jewish temple, then he will walk into the Most Holy Place and declare himself as God (Rev. 13:1-8; 2 Thess. 2:3-4).

The Bible does tell us exactly what makes him change. In Revelation 13:1, he is seen as the beast, having seven heads and ten horns. According to Revelation 17:8, these symbols belong to the beast in the bottomless pit, but it is clear that the man picks up these symbolic characteristics in Revelation 13, right in the middle of the seventieth week.

According to Revelation 17:8, this demon was on the

earth before, but in John's day he was locked in the bottomless pit. When it is time for this demon to come forth again, he will rule through his human counterpart (the Anti-christ). At that time he will become the eighth king (Rev. 17:11) in his encore appearance on the world scene. When he is released, he will go into perdition (destruction), possessing his human counterpart, making him the son of perdition.

The characteristics of the demon show up in the son of perdition (the Anti-christ) in the middle of the seventieth week. This demon must ascend out of the bottomless pit in order to possess his human counterpart, and as long as he is locked in the bottomless pit, it's impossible for him to do anything on the earth.

The bottomless pit is the *what* that is preventing the beast in the bottomless pit from entering into the man of sin, transforming him into the son of perdition. The *neuter* Greek word translated *what* is used in this passage (2 Thess. 2:6), not allowing for interpretation as a personage. Until the beast from the bottomless pit is released, the man of sin cannot be uncovered or revealed as the son of perdition.

There is absolutely no authority in this passage to interpret the *what* as the Holy Spirit. The reason normally given for this interpretation comes from the fact that Jesus referred to the Holy Spirit as "He, Him, and Himself" in John. However, in the Pauline Epistles, Paul uses the pronouns in reference to the Holy Spirit only when he has clearly identified the Holy Spirit in the text already. In this passage, expositors have only assumed the Holy Spirit is the one of whom Paul speaks.

I'm not saying that the Holy Spirit can't or never restrains evil. But, I am saying it is not the ministry of the Holy Spirit to literally restrain demons. And, demonic restraint is what is at issue in 2 Thessalonians 2:6-8. Now, it is clear why a thorough understanding of the tri-part personality of the beast, and where it is he's being detained, is essential for a correct interpretation of 2 Thessalonians 2.

Seven

❧❧ ❧❧

Identifying the "He" Who Now Letteth

As I stated in the last chapter, there have been numerous attempts to identify the *he* who now letteth, found in 2 Thessalonians 2:7. The most popular interpretation is that the word represents the Holy Spirit Himself. I was reading a book by one of the most renowned authors of pre-trib rapture theory, who, commenting on the *he* found in the above passage, uses Genesis 6:3 as a proof text, where the Lord says, "My Spirit shall not always strive with man."

I thought to myself, as true as this Scripture is, it sure isn't a good text to prove the restraining ministry of the Holy Spirit. Then I did some more research and looked up all the Scriptures I could find concerning the Holy Spirit, and I couldn't find one solid Scripture that actually says the Holy Spirit has a "restraining ministry."

As I read other commentaries and exegeses concerning the identity of the *he*, I could find only personal conclusions. "It can be no other than . . ." or "Who else is able to restrain the revealing of the son of perdition . . ." were the speculative phrases I found. This perplexed me further, because I noticed the consistent absence of Scripture that actually proved their point. The basic tenets of the question "who else is able to restrain the revealing of the son of perdition?" assumes that no one can but God. But, is this really true?

I remember back some years ago when I watched the space epic, *Star Wars*, where God was portrayed as both the Light Side and the Dark Side. The same god was both good and evil, equally divided between the two. As I stated in chapter 3, there are two kingdoms at war. Paul described this eloquently in his defense before King Agrippa: "To open their eyes and to turn them from darkness to light, and from the power of Satan unto God." These kingdoms are quite opposite but, contrary to *Star Wars*, not close to being equal. They are not an equally divided whole but two separate kingdoms. After Satan's failed heavenly coup attempt, the devil and his legions of fallen angels became the ambassadors of the kingdom of darkness, setting up Satan as the ultimate personification of wickedness in the universe. He is, nonetheless, limited. Remember, the devil is not omnipresent (everywhere at once), nor is he omniscient (all-knowing), and he certainly isn't omnipotent (all-powerful).

God created Lucifer who became the devil. Satan has never been a match for God. God the Holy Spirit does not have to personally restrain the devil, nor demonic spirits, Himself. Satan is a fallen *angel*, and God has committed the restraint of demons and Satan to the holy angels.

The Ministry of Angels

In Revelation 20:1-3, we witness an interesting encounter between Satan and one of God's holy angels:

And I saw an angel, come down from heaven, having the key of the bottomless pit and a great chain in his hand. And he laid hold on the dragon, that old serpent, which is the Devil, and Satan, and bound him a thousand years. And cast him into the bottomless pit, and shut him up, and set a seal upon him, that he should deceive the nations no more, till the thousand years should be fulfilled: and after that he must be loosed a little season. (Rev. 20:1-3)

Look at Satan! The god of this present world, the prince and the power of the air, grabbed, bound, and chained by one angel! Satan, the chief of all demonic spirits and evil principality and power, was no match for the angel who holds the key to the bottomless pit.

Now if Satan can be bound and chained, then cast into the bottomless pit for a predetermined amount of time, so can any other demon. If Satan can be rendered completely powerless by setting a seal on him, then so can any other demon. If Satan can be locked in the bottomless pit, without chance of escape, then so can any other demon. If Satan must be loosed before he can ascend or leave the bottomless pit, then so must any other demon.

This is the same bottomless pit from which the beast will ascend. It is highly unlikely that the beast is receiving any special privileges; I seriously doubt that the beast has his own key to the bottomless pit and can come and go as he pleases. It is also not probable that he is enjoying himself, as if on vacation, in this fiery place of detention. The beast, like the rest of the demons in the pit, is no doubt under chains. Before demons go in or come out of the bottomless pit, they must go past the angel who holds the key. This angel (or angels) has the responsibility for the literal restraint of the demons doing time in the pit.

God Himself determines when these demons are to be locked up and gives the order according to His own purposes. Just as a judge may order a bench warrant for a particular criminal, and the judge gives the authority to a deputy to pick him up, arrest, and detain him until his trial date comes, so it is with God and His angels.

The word *angel* comes from the Greek *angelos* and the Hebrew word *mal-awk*, both meaning "messenger" or "angel." Angelic beings are spirits of a supernatural order; they constitute a distinct order and are among the upper echelons of supernatural, created beings. Angels are immortal and are usually accredited with human characteristics. The more supernatural traits are strength, immense power, and wisdom. Angels carry out numerous tasks throughout the universe, including on the earth. An innumerable multitude go about doing the bidding of God. Their loyalties fall into two camps: God's holy angels and the devil and his angels. Another very interesting fact is angels are never referred to in the feminine but are always mentioned in the masculine.

Some of the tasks angels are charged with doing include: encamping around the saints of God, and serving the heirs of salvation (Ps. 34:7; Heb. 1:14); strengthening weakened human beings and encouraging them (Luke 22:43; Acts 27:23-24); fighting for and protecting humans using inconceivable, destructive powers (Ex. 23:20; 2 Kings 6:17; 19:35); and overseeing atmospheric conditions, celestial bodies, and wildlife (Rev. 7:1; 16:8; 19:17). These are just a few of their duties.

Other very important functions of angels are resisting and restraining demonic forces here on earth and in the heavenly realms. There are some well-documented cases of this in both Old and New Testaments. One of the most graphic accounts of an angelic/demonic war is found in Daniel 10. Daniel had prayed, and a holy angel was sent to him with the answer, but the angel had an encounter with the demonic ruler of the kingdom of Persia. Let's take a look at the passage, beginning at verse 12:

> Then *he* [the angel] said unto me, Fear not, Daniel:
> for from the first day that thou didst set thine
> heart to understand, and to chasten thyself before

> thy God, thy words were heard, and I am come for
> thy words. But the prince of the kingdom of Persia
> withstood me one and twenty days: but lo, Michael,
> one of the chief princes, came to help me; and I
> remained there with the kings of Persia. (Dan.
> 10:12-13) (emphasis mine)

Here is this angelic being, whose body had the appearance of beryl and a face that looked like lightning.
When Daniel saw this angel, he was shaken up so badly
that he lost all of his strength and fainted (vv. 6-11). This
is absolutely mind-boggling. Do you think a mere man
could have successfully withstood this awesome angel?
And yet, this angel was delayed three weeks by the demon
which ruled over the kingdom of Persia and needed back-
up from Michael the archangel. As you can see, these
angelic wars are serious!

At the close of Daniel 10, the angel makes an astounding statement:

> Knowest thou wherefore I come unto thee? and
> now will I return to *fight* with the prince of Persia:
> and when I am gone forth, lo, the prince of Grecia
> shall come. But I will shew thee that which is noted
> in the scripture of truth: there is *none* that *holdeth*
> with me in these things, but Michael the chief
> prince. (Dan. 10:20-21) (emphasis mine)

The word "holdeth" comes from the Hebrew word
khaw-zak, which means "to bind, restrain, or withstand."
Here we have an affirmation of the responsibility of angels to restrain these demonic principalities, coming from
the angel himself. As he says in the passage, there was
none who restrains with him but Michael, who is also an
angel. The Holy Spirit was neither mentioned nor referred to, in the least, as being the restraining force.

When Satan rebelled, he took one-third of the angels
with him (Rev. 12:4). Therefore, the holy angels out-num-
ber the demons by a two-to-one ratio. In this passage, we
see that the prince of the kingdom of Persia was double-

teamed. Paul also referenced these demonic principalities in Ephesians 6, where he says:

> For we wrestle not against flesh and blood [human beings] but against principalities, against powers, against the rulers of the darkness of this world, against spiritual wickedness in high places. (Eph. 6:12)

The word *high* means the lower heavenly realms. This is probably the realm where the demon withstood the angel in Daniel 10.

Another documented case of angelic restraint is found in Revelation 9. In this passage, the angel was sent to loose the four angels (demons) who were bound in the Euphrates River.

It is interesting to note the high amount of demonic activity in this part of the world. The Euphrates River runs through the plain of Shinar. It was in this ancient plain that Daniel was visited by the angel who was resisted by the prince of the kingdom of Persia. The plain of Shinar was the site of the tower of Babel, where the ancient city of Babylon was built. Today this territory is Iraq.

Another case of angels restraining evil spirits can be found in Jude 9; the passage says:

> Yet Michael the archangel, when contending with the devil he disputed about the body of Moses, durst [dared] not bring against him a railing accusation, but said, the Lord rebuke thee.

Whatever Satan's intentions for the body of Moses was, Michael was there to prevent it from happening. This passage also lets us know that the angels do not act independently of God. In this case Michael was doing the actual restraining, but the authority and the rebuke came from the Lord.

The final example of these angelic wars can be found

in Revelation 12:7. Michael and his angels fought against
the devil and his angels; and, again, no Holy Spirit was
mentioned. As I said before, I'm not suggesting at all that
the Holy Spirit can't or doesn't restrain evil or demons,
because the Holy Spirit is God, and nothing is impossible
with him. Although during the battle of Armageddon
Jesus Himself will fight, normally the restraint of the devil
and his demons is accomplished at an angelic level. The
holy angels are quite capable of handling God's light
work.

There are a three reasons I believe Paul uses the
pronoun *he:* (1) We don't know the names of the holy
angels, except for Michael and Gabriel; a clear example of
this can be found in Judges 13:17-18, which says: "And
Manoah said unto the angel of the Lord, What is thy
name, that when thy sayings come to pass we may do thee
honor? And the angel of the Lord said unto him, Why
askest thou thus after my name, seeing it is a secret?" God
obviously didn't feel it was necessary to reveal their names
to us; (2) Because angels are always referred to in the
masculine gender Paul's use of the pronoun *he* is appropriate; and (3) The use of the masculine is in harmony
with the rest of the Scriptures concerning angels.

Now you can see how the misinterpretation of these
three words, *he, what,* and *reveal* can change Christianity
for many people. As one of the best authorities on the
pre-trib rapture theory stated, "this passage (2 Thess. 2:3-
7) more than any other seems to validate the pre-trib
theory the best." If it were simply a matter of a wrong
interpretation with no negative ramifications, then it
wouldn't be a problem. But, this doctrine, resting upon
the sandy foundation of some bad interpretations of the
Scriptures, can be disastrous for Christians.

Eight

In His Time

In the great book of biblical poetry, Ecclesiastes, we find the well-known passage: "To everything there is a season, and a time to every purpose under the heaven." In the vast depth of God's purposes, we must come to understand there is an appointed time for everything.

We all come to the stark reality, at some point in our lives, that we must co-exist with evil. What's even harder to understand is that God has a purpose for evil, and He has determined a time and a place for it in His plans for the ages. On God's prophetic calendar of events, He has predetermined all things after the counsel of His own will. Unlike we earthly authors, who develop our schemes and themes as we go, God determines all things from the beginning and then brings them to pass. The prophet Isaiah says of God:

> I am God, and there is none like me, Declaring
> the end from the beginning, and from ancient

times the things that are not yet done, saying, My
counsel shall stand, and I will do all my pleasure.
(Isa. 46:9-10)

In this chapter, we shall take a look at the time God
has chosen to reveal the son of perdition.

Although many approach this subject as though prophetic events will just happen arbitrarily, most of us know
that is not true. Just because we don't know when prophetic events will occur doesn't mean that they're not
fixed according to God's timing. We may not have God's
time clock, but much of His schedule is written down for
us in His Word.

So, let's learn some more about the time that the
Lord has chosen to reveal the son of perdition, beginning
at 2 Thessalonians 2:5-6. The passage says:

Remember ye not, that, when I was yet with you,
I told you these things? And now ye know what
withholdeth that he might be revealed in his time.

From this passage and others we can understand that
there is a particular time for the revealing of the beast.
No matter how we interpret prophetic events, the time
for the revealing of the Anti-christ is set and cannot be
altered. As the Bible clearly teaches, whatever God has
purposed shall come to pass.

A perfect example of this can be seen in Revelation
17:16. The ten kings shall destroy the city of Babylon; and
yet, it is God who puts it in their hearts to fulfill His will.
Do you think it will be possible to change what is written?
Absolutely not!

In the two previous chapters, we covered the bottomless pit and the beast's relationship to it. We saw that the
Abyss is an escape-proof prison and a place of torment
for demonic spirits. However, these demons are allowed
to spend a predetermined amount of time on the earth
as well. As incredible as this may sound, there is reference to this in Matthew, Mark, and Luke.

In Matthew 8, we are introduced to the maniac of the Gadara. This crazed man was well known and feared by all in the region. He lived among the tombs and wore no clothes, because he was possessed with many demons. Attempts had been made to restrain him with chains and fetters, but he possessed superhuman strength and was able to break out of them.

When Jesus and His disciples approached this demoniac, the demons cried out, saying: "What have we to do with thee, Jesus, thou Son of God? art thou come hither to torment us before the time?" (Matt. 8:29). The question is a very interesting one. They weren't concerned with being tormented, but being tormented *before* it was time. These demons were obviously aware of their "time out of the pit" status, therefore they appealed to the Lord not to send them to the place of torment prematurely. Now, at first glance you might think that these demons were afraid of the final judgement to come, but they knew it wasn't time for that; it was something else which they feared.

In Mark we find this same account with a little more information. In Mark 5:9, it is said that this demon was called "Legion," a name that implies that there were many demons that had entered into this man. *Legion* is a military term that refers to troops, possibly consisting of six thousand soldiers. Can you imagine a person being possessed by thousands of demons?

In Luke, there is another account of this story. The good physician recounts how the demons beseeched Christ to let them possess a herd of swine, but not to command them to go out into the deep (Luke 8:31). At first, "the deep" may seem to refer to the water in which the pigs ended up drowning themselves, but it is not. The "deep" here is in reference to the bottomless pit—the feared place of torment. Both Jesus and the demons were aware that it was not time for the latter to be restrained in the Abyss, so Jesus allowed the evil spirits to possess a herd of swine on the mountainside nearby.

Forty-Two Months

As I have stated several times, thus far, in this book, the beast is only in his role for forty-two months. No matter who says differently, or how they try to stretch the Scriptures into saying something else, the Bible is very specific about this in both Old and New Testament accounts (Dan. 7:25; Rev. 13:5). In Daniel, it is noted that the daily sacrifice will be taken away in the middle of the seventieth week, which means the beast can only be in that role for the last half of the seventieth week.

In Revelation 11:2, we see that Jerusalem will be trodden down under the feet of the Gentiles (the kingdom of the beast) for a forty-two-month period. While the beast is in Jerusalem, ruling from God's throne, Israel's saved remnant will be nourished in the place prepared for them in the wilderness. They will kept "for a time, times, and half-a-time," or three-and-one-half years.

In the previous chapters, we saw that the man of sin cannot be revealed as the son of perdition until the "beast in the bottomless pit" is let out. This demon was on the world scene before, we learned, but in John's day, he was in the bottomless pit. He must therefore be released in the middle of the seventieth week according to God's prophetic time clock. To illustrate this point, we reference God's two witnesses, found in Revelation 11.

God's Two Witnesses

Beginning at verse 3, we are introduced to the two witnesses:

> And I will give power unto my two witnesses, and they shall prophesy a thousand, two hundred and threescore days. . . . These have power to shut heaven, that it rain not in the days of their prophecy: and have power over waters to turn them to blood, and to smite the earth with all plagues, as often as they will. (Rev. 11:3, 6)

No one is exactly sure who these two witnesses are. Some believe it will be Elijah and Moses, who met Jesus on the mount of transfiguration. Others believe that it will be Enoch and Elijah. Whoever they are, they're going to have a devastating prophetic ministry. They will be given great power to smite the earth as often as they want to, and no weapon formed will be able to prosper against them. The only limitation these prophets will have is a 1,260-day time period in which to carry out their mission on earth. This period is exactly three-and-one-half years (or forty-two, thirty-day months as in the Jewish calendar). This time coincides with the first half of the seventieth week.

After these two witnesses finish their allotted time to prophesy, verse 7 tells us what happens to them:

> And when they shall have finished their testimony, the beast that ascendeth out of the bottomless pit shall make war against them, and shall overcome them and kill them.

The Scriptures declare unequivocally that the beast is out of the bottomless pit when the two witnesses' days of prophecy are finished. It is absolutely impossible for this demon to fight them while still locked inside the pit—and we know that the beast is a demonic personality, not just some satanically inspired, governmental bureaucracy, as some interpret it—therefore, the Scriptures cleverly give the credit to "the beast out of the bottomless pit" to let us know that the demon is released by this time. After possessing the son of perdition, killing the two witnesses will be one of the first things the beast will do. This provides the beast (or Anti-christ) even greater, worldwide recognition, greater than the signing of the peace covenant. Verse 10 recounts a worldwide party honoring the beast for killing the two witnesses. After three-and-one-half days, God will raise them from the dead.

Then, according to Revelation 17:8, the earth's inhabitants shall wonder at the beast when they "behold, the beast that was, is not, and yet is." The world will admire the demonic charisma and power this human counterpart will now possess. Then they will say, "Who is like unto the beast? who is able to make war with him?" (Rev. 13:4). No one on earth will have been able to do away with the two witnesses, but the beast will bask in this great victory, setting the stage for his worldwide worship. The beast will forsake the "Holy Covenant" and take away the daily sacrifice, and thirty days later, he and the false prophet will place the abomination.

None of the actions of the beast can happen until the middle of the seventieth week. He (the son of perdition) cannot be revealed (uncovered) before the beast is let out of the bottomless pit, which will not happen before "his time." This is why the rider on the white horse, symbolized in Revelation 6, cannot technically be considered the beast. Again, the demon is only going to possess his human counterpart for the last three-and-one-half years, not all seven years of the seventieth week. It can happen only as God has purposed it to come to pass.

It is the same man the entire seventieth week, but he will only be the beast for forty-two months. In his "man of peace" persona, Israel accepts him. In no way would she have accepted him if the characteristics he manifests in the second half of the week were revealed at the beginning.

Nine
ᘒᘒ ᘒᘒ

The Wrath of God
(Part I)

This is a very important chapter about the wrath of God, because there is a lot of confusion over when it begins. Being able to rightly divide the Word of God concerning this subject will help the student of prophecy determine the validity and errancy of men's opinions, exegeses, and biblical facts.

In 1 Thessalonians 5:2, 9, the Apostle Paul tells us that the Church is not appointed to God's wrath. This is a biblical fact and is not debatable. The problem that arises comes from the interpretation of the scriptural view of "wrath." The question we need to ask ourselves is this: Is the doctrine I prefer based solely on what the Scriptures actually say? Or does my doctrine depend on loosely associated scriptural interpretations?

One of the most popular doctrines on the rapture, the "pre-trib" theory, is based on many loosely associated interpretations of Scriptures. A basic tenet of this doctrine is that the whole seventieth week of Daniel *is* the wrath of God. Under close scriptural scrutiny, however, placing precept upon precept, line upon line, their doctrine and their arguments will not hold water.

Throughout history, God has poured out his wrath and indignation upon many peoples, nations, and lands. Sometimes his wrath has been expressed at a local level, and sometimes on a global scale. Nations that have been exceedingly prideful, wicked, and arrogant have met their fate under the mighty, righteous hand of God. History's greatest kingdoms, such as Babylon, Egypt, Medo-Persia, Greece, and Rome, have all tasted God's awesome power when He is angry with a sinful people. Although the world has witnessed what God can do, they haven't seen the likes of what is to come when the final moment of judgment comes. Both Old and New Testament prophets write about a coming day of wrath, known as the day of the Lord. There has never been an outpouring of divine wrath of the magnitude of this coming day, the finale of all future prophetic events of this present age, with cataclysmic effects in both the heavenly and earthly realms. Isaiah's prophecy concerning this awful time of judgment is as follows:

> Behold the day of the Lord cometh, cruel both with wrath and fierce anger, to lay the land desolate: and he shall destroy the sinners thereof out of it. For the stars of heaven and the constellations thereof shall not give their light; the sun shall be darkened in his going forth, and the moon shall not cause her light to shine. . . . Therefore I will shake the heavens, and the earth shall remove out of her place, in the wrath of the Lord of hosts, and in the day of his fierce anger. (Isa. 13:9-10, 13)

All creation will feel the effects of the day of the Lord. In verse 9, Isaiah is also careful to inform us that the time of God's wrath will be during the day of the Lord. It's very important that I re-emphasize the close association between the day of the Lord and the wrath of God; it is the time period called the "day of the Lord" during which the wrath of God is poured out upon the earth.

The word *day* in the phrase "day of the Lord" may lead one to think that it is only in reference to a literal, twenty-four-hour day. Indeed, there will be an actual day when the Lord physically returns to the earth to fight in the battle of Armageddon. But, this is not the only connotation of the word *day* in this phrase. We shall study the day of the Lord in terms of the *time period* when God pours out His divine wrath on the earth.

The word *day* is translated from the Hebrew: *yowm* or *yome*. This word refers to a normal day—from sunrise to sunset, or a twenty-four-hour day. *Yome*, however, can also refer to a period of time. In reference to the latter definition, the day of the Lord will be a considerable period of time, to occur after the abomination of desolation is put in place. Specific signs will proceed its occurrence, referred to as the "cosmic disturbances."

The best way to gain a clear understanding of the day of the Lord is to follow its consistent themes throughout the Old and New Testaments.

The Wrath of God

The prophet Isaiah informs us that the day of the Lord is the day of God's wrath. "Behold the day of the Lord cometh, cruel both with wrath and fierce anger" (Isa. 13:9). The same theme is echoed by Zephaniah in chapter 1 of his prophecy.

> The great day of the Lord is near, it is near . . .
> even the voice of the day of the Lord . . . That day
> is a day of wrath, a day of trouble and
> distress. (Zeph. 1:14-15)

The association between the day of the Lord and the day of wrath is clear.

In the New Testament, this same theme is also characterized. For example, in 1 Thessalonians 5:2, 9, Paul says:

> For yourselves know perfectly that the day of the Lord so cometh as a thief in the night. For God has not appointed us to wrath, but to obtain salvation by our Lord Jesus Christ.

Again the association between the day of the Lord and the wrath of God is established, this time in the writings of Paul. The apostle's statement in verse 9 is important. It establishes the fundamental fact that the Church will not have to experience the wrath of God.

When one considers that all born-again believers throughout the ages make up the ecclesia, or the "true Church," which is the Body of Christ, it is clear why we are not appointed to God's wrath. Jesus Christ stood in and bore God's wrath for us upon His body on the cross, as is poignantly portrayed in Isaiah 53:4-5, 10:

> Surely he hath borne our griefs, and carried our sorrows. . . . But he was wounded for our transgressions, he was bruised for our iniquities: the chastisement of our peace was upon him; and with his stripes we are healed. . . . It pleased God to bruise him, he hath put him to grief: when thou shalt make his soul an offering for sin . . .

The prophet says that it pleased God to bruise Christ and to make His soul an offering for sin. God poured His wrath out on His Son while He hung on the cross. This is why Jesus prayed three times in the garden of Gethsemane to let the cup (full of divine wrath) pass from Him (Matt. 26:39). Jesus knew that God the Father would turn Christ into sin for us and make Him a curse for us, too (2 Cor. 5:21; Gal. 3:13). God rejected and forsook His Son as He hung on the cross; because, as it says in Habakkuk 1:13,

> Thou art of purer eyes than to behold evil, and canst not look upon iniquity.

God separated Himself from Christ, and Jesus tasted death (separation) for every man. In Matthew, we see that even the sun refused to shine upon Christ while God's wrath was being poured out on Him. Jesus cried out with a loud voice, "My God, my God, why has thou forsaken me?" (Matt. 27:45-46). "It is finished," He said in the end, and Jesus gave up the ghost, and the salvation of the world was completed (John 19:30; Luke 23:46).

While Jesus was on the cross, He tasted both spiritual and physical death for every man (Heb. 2:9). As a man, He died, physically bearing the sin of the world on His body; but, as the Son of God, He stepped through the corridors of time and tasted eternal separation for every man as well. Therefore, the Church, who is the spiritual "Body of Christ" (Eph. 1:22-23) will not have to bear the wrath of God again, because Jesus paid our debt in full.

The Abomination of Desolation

In Matthew 24, Jesus gives us a glimpse into the future in His Mount Olivet discourse; He reveals some of the world conditions that will be prevalent preceding His second advent.

> When ye therefore shall see the abomination of desolation, spoken of by Daniel the prophet, stand in the holy place, (whoso readeth, let him understand). (Matt. 24:15)

In this passage, Jesus refers to the abomination of desolation as a direct, prophetic signpost, signaling the coming of the day of the Lord. In verses 16-20, Jesus delivers parenthetical instructions to those who will be living in Israel during this time period. Then, in verse 21, He picks up the main thought again and tells us what the sighting of the abomination of desolation will mean.

> For then [after the abomination of desolation is set up], shall be great tribulation, such as was not since the beginning of the world to this time, no, nor ever shall be. (Matt. 24:21)

After the abomination of desolation is in place, Jesus exhorts there will come an unprecedented time of great tribulation, such as the world has never known! Since the abomination of desolation will be in place, this tribulation can only occur midway through the seventieth week of Daniel.

One of a Kind

The characteristics of this great time of trouble are noted by Jesus as being a time of trouble like one that has never been, nor shall ever be. This is a "one of a kind" event. In Mark 13, we see the same statement repeated just a little differently:

> For in those days shall be affliction such as was not from the beginning of creation which God created unto this time, neither shall be. (Mark 13:19)

In the Old Testament, both major and minor prophets wrote about this time of unprecedented upheaval. In Daniel 12:1, it says:

> And there shall be a time of trouble, such as never was since there was a nation even to that same time.

Also in Daniel 11:36-45, it is interesting to note that we are given a view of the beast (the human monarch) and his many exploits and confrontations:

> And the king shall do according to his will; and he shall exalt himself, and magnify himself above every god, and shall speak marvelous things against the God of gods, and shall prosper till the indignation be accomplished: for that that is determined shall be done. (Dan. 11:36)

This is exactly what Paul describes in 2 Thessalonians 2:4. Verse 1 of Daniel 12 begins with the word *and*. This means that chapter 12 is a continuation of chapter 11, and because we know unequivocally that this is talking about the beast, therefore the setting in this passage of

Scripture is past the middle of the seventieth week. This also means the abomination of desolation is already in place, because the beast is already exalting himself above all gods. Therefore, Daniel records the same theme in his prophecy, coinciding with Jesus' words and placing this time of trouble after the abomination of desolation is in place.

Joel also records this theme in his prophecy:

> For the day of the Lord cometh, it is nigh at hand.... There hath not been ever the like, neither shall be any more after it, even to the years of many generations. (Joel 2:1-2)

Joel uses the same theme as Jesus and Daniel do, referring to the time period, as well as a horrible army; however, Joel goes a step further by identifying this period of awesome trouble as the day of the Lord. The day of the Lord, or the time of God's wrath, is to be the time period which will never be repeated again nor equaled in severity. So Jesus, Daniel, Zephaniah, Joel, and the Apostle Paul were all speaking of the exact same time period.

Now there are many who claim that the entire seventieth week of Daniel is the wrath of God. Their conclusions are based on their own perceptions of what they consider wrath to be, not what Scripture says. The day of the Lord will occur where God has placed it on His prophetic calendar; yet some are determined to assign whatever time period they want to the wrath of God simply to back up their doctrines.

During the first half of the seventieth week, there will be many calamitous events occurring all over the world. As Jesus Himself says in Matthew 24:6-8:

> And ye shall hear of wars and rumors of wars: see that ye be not troubled: for all these things must come to pass, but the end is not yet. For nation shall rise against nation, and kingdom against kingdom: and there shall be famines, and pestilences, and earthquakes, in divers places. All these are the beginning of sorrows.

In this passage we are warned that all of these calamities, disastrous events, and natural catastrophes are just the beginning—symptoms of the coming day of the Lord, which will be much worse.

The Four Horsemen of the Apocalypse

In Revelation 6, we find the "four horsemen," beginning with the white horse and its rider in verse 2. This is the man of sin, who begins the seventieth week by introducing limited peace to the Middle East. This is not to say that the entire world will be free of war, but his political theme will be a peaceful one, and many will temporally benefit from it.

In verse 4, the red horse comes on the scene to take away the peace from the earth, and men shall kill one another. This parallels what Jesus said in Matthew 24: "nation shall rise against nation, kingdom against kingdom" (nation refers to ethnic groups).

The black horse arrives on the scene in verse 5. This horse represents famine, both economic and agricultural, occurring as a result of the war-stricken planet.

Last but not least, death and hell accompany the pale horse, gorged on the massive carnage from famine, war, pestilence, and disease. Hell widens its borders. Verses 5-8, coincide with what Jesus said, "there shall be wars and rumors of wars . . . there shall be famines and pestilence and earthquakes. These are but the beginning of sorrows."

The Seven Seals Opened

In Revelation 5, John records a scene in heaven, concerning the opening of a book with seven seals. As scrolls containing important messages were sealed with wax to prevent tampering, so was this significant document. Only one who was authorized to read the scroll could break the seals, and the same was true of this book.

Beginning at the second verse, there is a declaration heralded throughout heavens, asking: Who is worthy to open up the book, and to loosen the seals on it? No man in heaven, earth, nor under the earth, concludes verse 3, is worthy to open the book nor to even look at it. John wept because of this travesty of humanity. One of the elders informs John that the Lion of the tribe of Judah has prevailed to open the book and to loosen the seals.

Who was this one who was worthy to open the book and to look at it? Well, the answer to that question is found in Revelation 4:11:

> Thou art worthy, O Lord, to receive glory and
> honour and power: for thou has created all things,
> and for thy pleasure they are and were created.

The word *worthy* comes from the Greek *ax-ee-os*, which means "deserving or due reward." In this verse, worthiness was attributed to the Lord because He was the creator of all things. The one who was worthy, the Lord, had also prevailed to open and look at the book (Rev. 5:5). *Prevailed* comes from the Greek *nik-ah-o*, which means "to get the victory over something." This passage references Jesus' earthly ministry as the Lion of the tribe of Judah, the Root of David, the true King of the Jews.

So what does all of this mean? These passages identify the Lord as the only one who is worthy to open the book. *Worthiness* is the criterion. In addition to the fact that He had created all things, He also prevailed to open the book because He was the Lamb of God and the Lion of the tribe of Judah, who purchased and cleansed the whole creation with His own blood. He obtained victory over sin, death, and hell; this is why He was worthy and prevailed to open the book.

Now many people interpret these passages and use them to declare that the wrath of God begins with the opening of the first seal. Since the Lord opened the book, they say, it's obviously His wrath. The Scriptures are not saying that at all. The focus here is *worthiness* to open the book, not on the question of when the wrath begins. Jesus earned the right to open the book because He prevailed to open it; additionally, because He was the creator of all things, He is certainly worthy.

When one looks at the book of Revelation, one must consider that much of these obscure visions are similar to looking into a kaleidoscope. A dictionary definition of the term, *kaleidoscope*, is "continually changing and shifting from one set of relations to another; or rapidly changing; extremely complex and varied." Although some of Revelation is systematic, a lot of it isn't.

A good example of the kaleidoscopic nature of Revelation appears in chapters 4 and 5. In Revelations 4:8-11, the Lord is seen seated on the throne, being referred to as Lord God Almighty, who created all things. In 5:1, He has the book no man can open in His hand. Next, the Lord is seen as "the Lion from the tribe of Judah" who prevails to open the book. Then, it identifies Him as the Lamb that was slain. My point is: all three visions are of the same Lord, rapidly switching from image to another, all in the same vision. Such is the great kaleidoscope of Revelation.

Paul's Version of the Abomination of Desolation

One of the great aspects about the Holy Scriptures is the way God laid them out. One really doesn't have to struggle with interpreting a single passage in its own entity, because there are more passages elsewhere in the Bible which will either enhance it or clarify it. Considering this, we will take a look at the abomination of desolation through the eyes of Paul.

Although many may not be aware that Paul talks about the abomination of desolation, the fact is 2 Thessalonians 2 gives us some very specific details about it. Just as Jesus said in the gospels of Matthew (24:15, 21) and Mark (13:14, 19) that the day of the Lord would follow the abomination of desolation, the Apostle Paul does the same in his second letter to the Thessalonians.

In 2 Thessalonians 2:3, Paul clearly references two things that must occur before the day of the Lord. The first was the apostasy, or the falling away. The second was the man of sin being revealed or uncovered as the son of perdition. In the next verse, Paul describes "what is to be revealed." Speaking of the son of perdition, he says:

> Who opposeth and exalteth himself above all that is called God, or that is worshiped; so that he as God sitteth in the temple of God, shewing himself that he is God.

Since I have already covered in detail what it was to be revealed or uncovered relating to the son of perdition, who is also the beast; here, I will do a short review.

(1) There are three aspects of the beast: his kingdom, the person, and the demon in the bottomless pit (Dan. 7:7-8, 24, 25; Rev. 13:1-3; 17:8).

(2) The demon must be released from the bottomless pit in order to possess his human counterpart, this occurring in the middle of the seventieth week (Rev. 17:8,11; 11:3,7).

(3) At the time of the demon's release, the man of sin (also the rider of the white horse) picks up the symbolic characteristics of the demon (i.e., seven heads and ten horns) (Rev. 6:2 with 2 Thess. 2:3, "man of sin"; Rev. 13:1-5, "human," with 17:8, "the demon," now together).

(4) The beast begins his forty-two-month reign by blaspheming and openly opposing God (Dan. 7:8,25; 9:27; 11:36; Rev. 13:5).

(5) The beast places the abomination of desolation and calls himself God (Dan. 9:27; 11:31; Matt. 24:15; Mark 13:14; Rev. 13:14-15).

What Paul says about the son of perdition matches perfectly with the rest of the Scriptures. When the man of sin is uncovered as the son of perdition, he will blaspheme God. Therefore Paul asserts:

A) It's the son of perdition "who opposeth and exalts himself above all that is called God." This matches with point 4 above.

B) It's the son of perdition who enters the Holy Place,

sets up his image, and calls himself God. This matches
with point 5 above.

C) Paul realized that before the man of sin could be
uncovered as the son of perdition, the restraints placed
by the angel (the *he*) with the key to the bottomless pit
would have to be withdrawn. Additionally, the bottomless
pit (the *what*) would have to be opened before the demon
could ascend out of the bottomless pit. All this agrees
with points 1, 2, and 3.

How could the wrath of God start before the abomination of desolation has occurred? The king of this final
Gentile kingdom must be in place before God can respond in wrath to the beast's overt blasphemies and des-
ecration of the Holy Place. Remember the beast is only
the beast for forty-two months, which is the second half
of the seventieth week. Thus, Paul says that the day of the
Lord will not happen until the occurrence of the falling
away and the abomination of desolation, and he is consistent with Jesus and the prophets. If Paul was suggesting
that the day of the Lord took place at the beginning of
the seventieth week, his writings would contradict the rest
of the Scriptures. Therefore, none of the things he describes in 2 Thessalonians 2:4 occur at the beginning of
the week—not one!

In Daniel 9:27, we read,

> And for the overspreading of abominations, *he*
> [the son of perdition, or Anti-christ] shall make *it*
> [the holy place] desolate, even until the consum-
> mation [the completion of his iniquity] and that
> determined [God's wrath] shall be *poured* [see Rev.
> 16, the seven vials] upon the desolate [the desola-
> tor, or the beast]. (emphasis mine)

It is impossible for verse 27 to be fulfilled in the
beginning of the week prior to the beast initiating his
forty-two-month reign, which doesn't start until the middle
of the seventieth week.

Blood on the Moon

In Matthew 24:29, Jesus says:

> Immediately after the tribulation of those days shall
> the sun be darkened, and the moon shall not give
> her light, and the stars shall fall from heaven, and
> the powers of heaven shall be shaken.

Jesus said, "Immediately after the tribulation of those
days. . . ." What tribulation is he talking about? He is
referring to the tribulation to come upon the Jews and
the rest of the world after the middle of the seventieth
week. Remember, Israel will be a land of unwalled villages
and safe dwelling in the land (Ezek. 38:8, 11). The covenant of peace will have already been enacted, but in the
middle of the week, just as the people are commenting
on "peace and safety" (1 Thess. 5:3), the beast will emerge
out of the bottomless pit and be revealed in the son of
perdition. He will then remove the daily sacrifice and
place the abomination of desolation.

He will also declare himself as God and persecute
every saint (the Church and Israel) whom he can get his
hands on (Dan. 7:25; Rev. 12:13-17; 13:7). This time of
great tribulation, as it relates to the persecution of the
saints, will last until God kicks in *His* wrath. This is why
Jesus said, And when you see the abomination of desolation . . . flee into the mountains. According to Daniel
12:11, it will take the beast thirty days to set up the
abomination after he removes the daily sacrifice. Then
the 2 Thessalonians 2 scenario will commence. The beast
will declare himself as God and endeavor to kill all who
refuse to worship him as God. The Bible does not specify
how long he will persecute believers.

God will respond suddenly to the beast's blasphemies
in an unprecedented outpouring of his fierce wrath, as
noted in Luke 21:25, 28, quoting Jesus:

> And there shall be signs in the sun, and in the
> moon, and in the stars; and upon the earth dis-
> tress of nations, with perplexity the sea and the

waves roaring. . . . And when these things begin to
come to pass, then look up, and lift up your heads;
for your redemption draweth nigh.

Where Jesus says, "And when you begin to see these
things come to pass . . ." he is referring to the signs in the
sun and the moon and the stars. Throughout the Scriptures, these cosmic signs are part of the day of the Lord
scenario. Isaiah 13:9-10, Zephaniah 1:14-15, Zechariah 14:6-
7, and Amos 5:18-20 all write of these horrifying, cosmic
disturbances. Each one of these prophets tells us that
these signs occur as part of the day of the Lord. However,
Jesus told us that when we begin to see these things, we
are to look up. Does that mean that the Church will enter
the day of the Lord, the day of God's wrath? Absolutely
not! The reason is in the second chapter of Joel's prophecy. Beginning at verse 31, the prophet says:

> The sun shall be turned into darkness, and the
> moon into blood before that great and terrible
> day of the Lord come.

Jesus exhorted believers to look up, "for your redemption draws nigh." What redemption is this? Jesus
has already died on the cross for our sins when this
comes to pass, so that aspect of redemption is already
completed. The answer can be found in Hebrews 9:28:

> So Christ was once offered to bear the sins of
> many; and unto them that look for him shall he
> appear the second time without sin unto salvation.

And, Paul says in Titus 2:13:

> Looking for that blessed hope, and the glorious
> appearing of the great God and our Saviour Jesus
> Christ . . .

And John adds a look at this blessed hope in 1 John
3:2-3, which says:

> Beloved, now are we the sons of God and it doth
> not yet appear what we shall be: but we know that,

when *he shall appear*, we shall be like him; for we shall see him as he is. And every man that hath this *hope* in him purifieth himself even as he is pure. (emphasis mine)

The redemption of which Christ spoke (Luke 21:28) is the redemption of our bodies (Rom. 8:21-23); this is the rapture. Paul told us the same thing: We are not appointed to the day of the Lord, the day of His wrath (1 Thess. 5:2, 9). These signs appear in the heavens before the day of the Lord comes.

Although these signs do occur prior to the commencement of the day of the Lord, they will also continue to appear straight through it, as well. This can be seen from the accounts of the prophets Amos and Zechariah regarding the day of the Lord. In Amos 5:18, 20, the prophet says:

Woe unto you that desire the day of the Lord! To what end is it for you? the day of the Lord is darkness, and not light. Shall not the day of the Lord be darkness, and not light? even very dark, and no brightness in it?

Here, the prophet Amos tells us that this whole time period will be darkness, with no light in it at all. The prophet Zechariah adds in chapter 14 of his prophecy:

And it shall come to pass in that day, that the light shall not be clear, nor dark: But it shall be one day which shall be known to the Lord, not day nor night: but it shall come to pass, that at the evening time it shall be light. (Zech. 14:6-7)

Zechariah provides some more details to the day of the Lord, specifically, that the days and nights will not be clear. Remember that Jesus said no man would be able to know the day or the hour of His return. It is because the sun and moon will not be in their normal rotations! The very celestial bodies that the Lord placed in the heavens to measure time will be sufficiently altered to disrupt days and hours (Gen. 1:14, 18). This is why Jesus said:

Men's hearts failing them for fear, and for looking
after those things which are coming on the earth:
for the powers of heaven shall be shaken. (Luke
21:11, 25-26)

Jesus knew that men wouldn't be able to predict the
day or the hour either of His return for the Church or
His return to earth in His second advent. The hour represents the exact time of His return, and the day represents the actual day of His return. In either case, due to
the cosmic disturbances and the retardation of their respective rotations, neither day nor hour will be predictable.

Some also have said, "How could the day of the Lord
come as a thief in the night when it is preceded by the
cosmic signs?" Well, first of all, we don't know how long
the cosmic disturbances will be visible before God's wrath
actually commences. It could be days, weeks, or months.
Secondly, according to Daniel 12:10:

but the wicked shall do wickedly: and NONE of
the wicked shall understand. (emphasis mine)

Paul also tells us that God will be turning the wicked
over to "strong delusion" (2 Thess. 2:11-12), so that the
unrighteous will believe a lie. The wicked will not have
understanding to determine the exact prophetic significance of what they will see in the heavens. But, when the
wrath of God begins to be poured out, they will cry out,
"hide us from the face of him that sitteth on the throne,
and from the wrath of the Lamb" (Rev. 6:16-17).

Ten

❧❧ ❧❧

The Wrath of God (Part II)

❧❧❧❧❧❧❧ ❧❧❧❧❧❧❧

The thing one always needs to keep in mind is the day of the Lord is a period of time that has never been, nor will ever be again. There is only one day of the Lord where God pours out his divine wrath in the horrible bowl judgments of Revelation 16. In the last chapter, I described the book of Revelation as being very kaleidoscopic. I believe, and I will attempt to demonstrate, that this same principle holds true when it comes to the wrath of God.

Beginning with Revelation 6:14, John says:

> And the heaven departed as a scroll when it is rolled together; and every mountain and island were moved out of their places. And the kings of the earth, and the great men, and the rich men,

and the chief captains, and the mighty men, and
every bondman, and every free man, hid themselves in the dens and in the rocks of the mountains; And said to the mountains and rocks, Fall
on us, and hide us from the face of him that sitteth
on the throne, and from the wrath of the Lamb;
For the great day of his wrath is come: and who
shall be able to stand? (Rev. 6:14-17)

From this text we can see that, without a doubt, the
day of the Lord is what is in view. In Revelation 11, we
can also detect a glimpse of the wrath of God, when the
seventh trumpet sounds. "And the nations were angry,
and thy wrath is come" (Rev. 11:18). But, this isn't all.
Chapter 16 depicts for us God's wrath rationed into seven
vials or bowls (Rev. 16:1-21).

The Great Kaleidoscope

Since there are different references to the wrath of
God, now the question is: Are there different "wraths" of
God? A wrath of God for the sixth seal? A wrath of God
for the seventh trumpet? Yet another wrath of God for
the vials of Revelation 16? Anybody would be scratching
his or her head about now, but I urge, relax; it's not as
difficult as it seems. Just remember what the Scriptures
tell us repeatedly: the day of the Lord is a one of a kind
event in all world history, and it will never be repeated
again.

These three scenarios which give context to the wrath
of God (the sixth seal, the seventh trumpet, and the seven
vials) are different kaleidoscopic visions of the same event.
The sixth seal is the *vision* of the wrath of God that is
actually poured out in chapter 16. The seventh trumpet
is where the *assumption* of the kingdoms of this world into
Christ's kingdom is announced, setting the stage for the
wrath to commence (there will be more on this later).
Therefore, the wrath of God to *follow* is alluded to here
when the seventh trumpet sounds.

Again, there is only one time period in all of earth's
history where the day of the Lord will occur. To believe

that there is wrath under the seals, and wrath under the trumpets, and wrath under the bowls overlooks the consistent, scriptural theme that the event would be unique.

> Such as was not since the beginning of the world to this time, no, nor ever shall be. (Matt. 24:21)

One clear illustration of this point is the earthquake envisioned in Revelation 6:12, 14 at the opening of the sixth seal:

> There was a great earthquake; . . . and every mountain and island were moved out of their places.

Now, in Revelation 16, this great earthquake is depicted as occurring during the pouring out of the seventh bowl:

> And there was a great earthquake, such as was not since men were upon the earth, so mighty an earthquake, and so great . . . And every island fled away, and the mountains were not found. (Rev. 16:18, 20)

Since the theme of this chapter is the actual outpouring of the wrath of God, it provides more details about the event than the seventh trumpet or the sixth seal does. But, this *is* the same earthquake that was envisioned in chapter 6. Unfortunately, some of the eschatological arguments which have surfaced concerning the wrath of God are the result of interpreters appointing the grammatical complexities of the Greek and English language as the greatest authority in interpretation of texts. For example, some argue that the original Greek rendering means that wrath is actually occurring at the sixth seal; therefore, wrath begins with the seals.

There isn't a language on this planet that could adequately express the revelation of God's word perfectly. As humans (i.e., creatures), we are not perfect, and neither are any of our languages. God (i.e., the Creator) is perfect. If we give the analysis of grammar greater authority in interpretation of the Scriptures, rather than placing precept upon precept and line upon line, we will continue to have serious problems. Proverbs says: "I will pour out my spirit unto you, I will make known my words unto you" (Prov. 1:23). Daniel wrote: "Knowledge shall be increased." All of the Bible asserts that it is the ministry of the Holy Spirit to teach you (1 John 2:27), but many of us give preeminence to Greek grammar.

The Great Announcement

I stated earlier that I believe the seventh trumpet is very significant, and one subject I intend to cover at great length in upcoming chapters. One of the elements, apart of the blowing of this trumpet, is the announcement of: "The kingdoms of this world are become the kingdoms of our Lord and of his Christ!" (Rev. 11:15). This is an important key to understanding why the wrath of God commences after this announcement.

John 18:33-38 provides better insight on this passage:

> Then Pilate entered into the judgment hall again, and called Jesus, and said unto him, Art thou the King of the Jews? Jesus answered him, Sayest thou this thing of thyself, or did others tell it thee of me? Pilate answered, Am I a Jew? Thine own nation and the chief priests have delivered thee unto me: what hast thou done? Jesus answered, My kingdom is not of this world: if my kingdom were of this world, then would my servants fight, that I should not be delivered to the Jews: but now is my kingdom not from hence. (John 18:33-36)

Jesus told a representative of the world power of that day, Rome (the iron legs of Daniel 2), that if Christ's kingdom were of this world then the fight would be on. But now, my kingdom is not from here, said Jesus. In Luke 17:20-21, Jesus said that the kingdom comes without notice because "the kingdom of God is within you." During this church age, the Christian is not part of a fully visible kingdom; we are yet waiting for the "manifestation" of the sons of God (Rom. 8:18-23). Although the kingdom of God is come already in us, it has not yet come in full manifestation. We are awaiting the continuance and fulfillment of the Davidic Kingdom, when the Lord returns as King of kings and Lord of lords and rules the earth during the millennium. Then every one shall witness Him in His second advent.

Now, when Jesus said, "If my kingdom were of this world, then would my servants fight," do you think He was talking about the eleven disciples? Of course not! Remember, Jesus Himself stated, "For it is written, I will smite the shepherd, and the sheep of the flock shall be scattered abroad" (Matt. 26:31; Zech. 13:7). So He knew they would be overcome with fear and abandon Him.

A hint of whom the Lord was speaking can be found in Matt. 26:53. After Peter cut off the temple guard's ear, Jesus said: "Thinkest thou that I cannot now pray to my Father, and he shall presently give me more than twelve legions of angels?" If He would have done that, the Scriptures would not have been fulfilled. It wasn't time for the kingdoms of the world to come under the kingdom of our Lord and Christ in full manifestation. Therefore, there has been a delay in God's intervention of wrath, now for almost two thousand years.

But, according to Revelation, that will suddenly change. For in the days of the voice of the seventh trumpet, there should be delay no longer (Rev. 10:6-7). The door for the wrath of God to commence will open. During the seventh vial, the Lord Himself returns to the earth in full manifestation and glory, with all His saints, to fight in the battle of Armageddon and usher in His everlasting kingdom (Rev. 19:12-16; Dan. 2:44-45).

During this two thousand years (so far) of delay between the old Roman Empire (the iron legs) and the emergence of the reconstructed Roman Empire (the ten toes of iron and clay), God has been working out His agenda. One element was the mystery that was hidden for ages, the Church!

The Seven Vials of Wrath

To get a much closer view of the wrath of God, we must go to the fifteenth chapter of Revelation.

> And I saw another sign in heaven, great and marvelous, seven angels having the seven last plagues: for IN THEM, is FILLED UP the wrath of God. (Rev. 15:1) (emphasis mine)

In this passage, John tells us that the wrath of God is filled up in these last seven plagues (the seven vials)—not the other plagues, but in these. Notice also the use of the phrase "filled up" *in connection with the wrath of God.* The word *filled* comes from the Greek *tel-eh-o,* which has various meanings; for example: "To end, complete, execute, conclude, discharge, accomplish, make an end, expire, fill up, finish, go over, pay, and perform." Now from these many definitions, a few different implications can be drawn, but I will examine two. The first inference that can be drawn is *completion.* Using the thought of completion, the verse would read: "For in them is "completed" the wrath of God. The other definition, *filled up,* gives this verse another essence all together. *Filled up* infers fullness in volume, such as a gas tank would be. When we use the meaning *filled up,* it better amplifies the phrase "in them," which references the vials containing the wrath of God (Rev. 15:7).

The word *vial* comes from the Greek *fee-al-ay,* which means "a broad shallow cup or a bowl." Bowls hold volume and are therefore "filled up" with God's wrath, which is to be poured out upon the earth. I believe the translators of the King James Bible used "filled up" as opposed to "completion," because, according to this text, the object is the bowls or vials which are filled up the wrath of God. Therefore, God's wrath is executed or accomplished when it is poured out of the seven vials.

The next word I would like to examine is *plague.* *Plague* is translated from the Greek word *play-gay,* which means "a calamity." Now, because these seven vials are the last, does not mean that the plagues prior to this were also the wrath of God.

I once heard a famous proponent of the pre-trib position say: "You mean to tell me that the seven trumpets and the seals aren't God's wrath? If that's not the wrath of God, I don't know what is!" Well, the problem is that many of us, including eschatology "experts" don't know what the wrath of God is. They look at the trumpets and say, "Look at the terrible events that take place; this has to be the wrath of God." But, again, this is based on how they look at it and not on what the Bible is actually saying.

To shed light on how the last plagues (not the previous plagues) can be the wrath of God, I would like to draw an illustration from a professional basketball season. As most of us know, the NBA's season is divided up into three parts: the regular season games, the playoff games, and the championship games. Now in all three parts of the season, it's the same basketball game. In all three parts of the season, they still have to shoot the ball through the basketball hoop. In all three parts of the season, the object is to score the most points to win. These elements don't change.

Are the trumpets and vials all calamities or plagues? Yes! Do people die? Yes! Are terrible things happening in the earth's ecology? Yes! Just as in the basketball season, there are common factors in each segment of the season, but the championship games are not the regular season games. In the championship games the intensity of play is greater, the stakes are much higher, and the games are played specifically at the end of the season. The regular season games may lead up to the championship games, but they are not the championships, no matter what the similarities are. A player can only get a championship ring if he wins the championship series. No other game during the regular season will get him that championship ring, no matter how intense the game is, or how many points are scored. Only in the last games can a player earn champion status, for in them a player can become an NBA champion and wear the coveted championship ring!

To demonstrate this point, let's compare the seven trumpets with the seven vials.

The Seven Trumpets

In Revelation 8, we see the seven angels preparing to blow the trumpets, which will release the respective plagues. As we study each of these trumpets, a common theme will surface in each one of them.

The first angel sounded his trumpet, and one-third of the trees and all green grass were burned up. The second angel sounded, and one-third of the sea was turned into blood, and one-third of all the ships and marine life were destroyed. The third angel sounded his horn, and one-third of all rivers and fountains were poisoned by the star called Wormwood. The fourth angel sounded, and a one-third part of the sun and the moon was affected. The fifth angel sounded his trumpet, and demon locusts were released from the bottomless pit. They were forbidden to hurt any vegetation, but they were permitted to hurt men who didn't have the seal of God on their foreheads. They were allowed to torture these people for five months, but they were forbidden to kill them. The sixth angel sounded, and a demon-inspired army was prepared to slay a third part of men. I will be dealing with the seventh trumpet later.

Now as bad as these plagues are, they pale in comparison to the seven vials. Each one of these trumpets was restricted to affecting just one-third of their targets. Although one-third is a lot, two-thirds remaining is twice as much. I'm sorry, folks, that was just the playoffs.

The Championship Series Begins

Just as the level of intensity increases, from the regular season to the playoffs, only the greatest players can handle the extreme intensity of the championship games.

The magnitude of the seven trumpets cannot be compared with the seven vials. Remember, for in them (i.e., the vials) are filled up the wrath of God.

In Mark 13:19, Jesus spoke of the day of the Lord; the passage says:

> For in those days shall be affliction, such as was not from the beginning of the creation which God created unto this time, neither shall be.

Because Jesus repeats the prophetic theme above, we know that He is speaking of the day of the Lord. But, in verse 20, the Lord clearly tells us of the increased magnitude of the day of the Lord, heightened to such a degree that this day could never occur again. The passage says: "And except those days be shortened no flesh would be saved." The wrath of God during the day of the Lord will be so devastating that all humanity would be completely obliterated.

This couldn't have applied to the seven trumpets; their limitations alone (i.e., one-third) would exclude them from the possibility of being this devastating. When speaking of the day of the Lord, the prophet Isaiah says that "the earth would reel to and fro like a drunkard" (Isa. 24:20).

In keeping with the Old Testament prophets, Jesus' prophecies, and the writings of the Apostle Paul, John's book of the Revelation bears out the exact same truths as do the others. It is our responsibility to decipher the continuation of the theme.

In Revelation 16:2, we see "round one" of the championship series. The first angel poured out his vial, and a grievous and noisome sore fell upon all that had the mark of the beast. It is quite obvious that this scenario occurs beyond the middle of the seventieth week. The abomination of desolation, which is in the second half of the week, is in place, evidenced by the mark of the beast already being law. Subsequently, the image of the beast has to already have been placed in the temple's Most Holy Place.

The beast is obviously in power and has had time to make war with the saints (Rev. 13:1-8). Is it just a mere coincidence that the first round of the wrath of God starts after the middle of the seventieth week? No! Is it just a coincidence that the very first thing that the wrath of God targets is those with the mark of the beast? No! This unequivocally lines up with the rest of Scripture.

I wish a pre-trib proponent could show me just one passage of Scripture that positively asserts that, "that determined" (wrath) is poured out on the desolator (i.e., the beast; Dan. 9:27) at the beginning of the seventieth week. The reason why one can't is because this individual is not the beast until the middle of the seventieth week, when the beast is released from the bottomless pit. The wrath of God couldn't possibly be poured out on him before he becomes the beast. How can the wrath of God be poured out on him before he even takes over the ten-nation confederacy? This is why Paul said "that day" (the day of the Lord) can't come until the abomination of desolation occurs, when the beast walks into the Holy Place and sits on the throne of God declaring himself to be God. This abomination is a part of the increasing abomination(s) that maketh "it" (the Holy Place) desolate (Dan. 9:27; 2 Thess. 2:3-4).

The second angel poured out his vial on the sea, and every living creature in the sea died, not just a third. The third angel poured out his vial, and the rivers and fountains became blood; no mention is made of a restriction on the number. The fourth angel poured out his vial, and men were scorched with great heat. There won't be enough sun screen for this awful plague.

The fifth angel poured out his vial on the kingdom of the beast; it is said that they gnawed their tongues due to the pain. This plague will be worldwide (i.e., not restricted to a third), wherever the beast kingdom extends. The sixth angel poured out his vial, and demons gathered the world's kingdoms to fight in the battle of Armageddon.

And, the seventh angel poured out his vial, and the world's worst earthquake in the history of the planet leveled every major city in the world, including the city of Babylon (more on this later). The Richter scale won't have enough notches to measure this cataclysmic convulsion. On top of all of this, one-hundred-pound hail will fall from heaven. Compare this hail with the first trumpet's hail.

No matter how one looks at it, the wrath of God begins when the Scriptures say so, and that's after the abomination of desolation.

The good news is that the Church does not go through any part of the wrath of God. We will analyze this in detail in the next chapter.

Eleven

The Great Mysteries

As we continue in our study, this chapter is one that I take great pleasure in writing. The student of Bible prophecy will find the study of God's plans for the ages a very fulfilling one. It is absolutely amazing how God brings all of His design together according to His divine master plan, purposed before the world began.

A great deal of God's purposes have been revealed to us throughout the Bible. The prophets of old testified of the things commonly reported to us now, concerning the saving power of Jesus Christ. The Bible also tells us that all of those prophets and saints received a good report, but they died without receiving the promises. However, God provided some better thing for us (the Body of Christ), that they (the saints of old), without us, should not be made perfect (Heb. 11:39-40).

The Scriptures which I referenced above puzzled me for a long time. Why, I thought, couldn't these Old Testament saints and prophets be made perfect without the Church? Well, one day the Lord enlightened me in this way. He likened it to a relay race, where each man is responsible for his own leg of the race. Out of the five past dispensations, there were saints in each who faithfully ran their leg of the race. For their faithfulness, they obtained a good report. Just as in a relay race, once one has completed his leg of the race, it is time for him to rest. Well, the saints of old have done their part, now they rest (in heaven) and cheer on those who run the race today.

What this means is, until the last man makes it to the finish line, the whole relay team cannot share in the victory. They can only relish the victorious moments of their leg of the race. But, when the last man crosses the finish line, the whole team rejoices. Although the others share in the victory, only the anchor man actually completes the race. Likewise, Israel has passed the baton to the Gentile church, which is "the Body of Christ," and the Church shall cross the finish line.

This was always God's plan for the ages, but until the resurrection of Christ, God's agenda was shrouded in great clouds of mystery, kept a secret since the foundation of the world. The long delay between Christ's two advents will be finished at the sounding of the seventh trumpet. Let's take a look at the passage where this is found. In Revelation 10:6–7, an angel makes an astounding declaration:

> And swear by him that liveth forever and ever, who created heaven, and the things that therein are, and the earth, and the things that therein are, and the sea, and the things which are therein, that there should be time no longer: But in the days of the voice of the seventh angel, when he shall begin to sound, the mystery of God should be finished, as he hath declared to his servants the prophets.

This passage of Scripture is extremely important. The seventh trumpet signals the completion of God's mystery.

During the summer of 1993, while I was at the Milwaukee Rescue Mission, I was teaching from my book to some students of Maranatha Bible College. During this lesson on God's mysteries, my friend, Nate, brought in a commentary by Dr. John Rice on the book of Revelation. I turned to his commentary on the tenth chapter of Revelation, and when I read it, I must admit I laughed.

Unfortunately, Dr. Rice said that the mystery in Revelation 10 was in reference to the day of the Lord. I thought to myself, "Boy, where did he get that from?" The day of the Lord is not a mystery! As a matter of fact, it is plainly declared throughout the Old Testament.

In my opinion, his conclusions were related to his pre-trib position. What I mean is this: Pre-tribers believe the Church will already be raptured from the earth (ref. Rev. 4:1). According to that doctrine, there is no so-called mention of the Church in Revelation beyond chapter 3. Therefore, Dr. Rice as well as other pre-tribers cannot see the significance of this passage to the Church (ref. Rev. 10:6-7).

It is similar to a radar programmed to scan only at a low altitude. Everything above the pre-set range will not register on the radar screen. Although a contact may in fact be there, it's just not seen because of an inadequate radar program. I will be covering what I believe is the pre-trib lack of insight in my chapter, "Why They Can't See the Church," later.

Dr. Rice's interpretation of "the mystery of God" as the day of the Lord is quite indicative of the negative effects pre-trib doctrine has had on the analysis of a lot of important Revelation passages. Several passages do indeed pertain to the Church of Jesus Christ. But, because of pre-trib presuppositions, many very important passages are passed over and given frivolous interpretations.

The word which is translated mystery comes from the Greek *moos-tay-ree-on*, which means "a secret, or the hidden counsel of God," unknown to man except by divine revelation. The question is: Why is the consummation of God's mystery so relevant to us today? We shall study this question in great detail.

To get a good handle on the mystery of God, we must begin our study in Romans 11:25, which says:

> For I would not, brethren, that ye should be igno-
> rant of this mystery, lest ye should be wise in your
> own conceits; that blindness in part is happened
> to Israel, until the fullness of the Gentiles be come
> in.

Part of the reason for the national "blindness" of Israel concerning the rejection of Jesus Christ as their Lord and King was God's "secret agenda" concerning the salvation of the Gentiles. The Gentiles were to come into their fullness (or numerical completion), and then Israel's blindness would be lifted. Although the prophets of old did declare that the Gentiles would be saved, God didn't reveal how, when, or where He would bring this to pass. His plans for the Gentiles remained a mystery.

As we continue in our study, we shall detect a direct correlation between the fullness of the Gentiles and the Church which Jesus said He was going to build. In Matthew 16:16–18, Jesus references this church:

> And Simon Peter answered and said, Thou art the
> Christ, the Son of the Living God. And Jesus an-
> swered and said unto him, Blessed art thou, Simon
> Bar-jona: for flesh and blood hath not revealed it
> unto thee, but my Father which is in heaven. And
> I say also unto thee, That thou art Peter, and upon
> this rock I will build my church; and the gates of
> hell shall not prevail against it.

For the first time, Jesus begins to unfold the mystery that had been hidden for ages: the Church that He Him-self would build. The word "church" comes from the Greek *ecclesia*, which means "an assembly of called out ones." The Church had its beginning in Jerusalem (A.D. 33) on the day of Pentecost. The first members of this

Church were 120 Jews who had gathered together in the upper room (Acts 1:12-15; 2:1-5).

On this day, a miraculous fulfillment of prophecy took place. The Holy Spirit fell on the 120 assembled in the upper room. The Bible says the cloven tongues of fire rested upon those who were in the room, and they began to speak in other tongues (i.e., languages). In Jerusalem at the time were Jews from every nation who came each year to celebrate Pentecost. When these Jews heard the Holy Spirit-filled saints speaking to them in their native languages, many thought that the believers were drunk. They were amazed, saying, "Are not these Galileans? How is it that we hear them in our native languages?" (Acts 2:1-13). But then, Peter stood up and assured them: "For these are not drunken as ye suppose, seeing it is but the third hour of the day [9 A.M.]. But this is that which was spoken by the prophet Joel" (Acts 2:15-16).

What Jesus had announced to Peter in Matthew 16, had now begun fulfillment on the day of Pentecost. The Church's miraculous birth was the fulfillment of a prophecy declared by the prophet Joel (Joel 2:28-32). Yes, the keys to the kingdom that Jesus gave to Peter were first used on the Jews (Matt. 16:19). However, at this point, the gospel was primarily to the Jews only.

As we continue in the Book of Acts, God begins to further unfold His mystery. In Acts 10, Peter sees a vision that would change his ministry and Christian history forever. In this vision Peter saw a sheet being let down from heaven. On this sheet were all sorts of ceremonial unclean animals, unfit for Jewish consumption. Peter then heard the Lord say, "kill and eat," but Peter replied, "Not so Lord, for I have never eaten any thing that is common or unclean." Then the Lord said to Peter, "What God hath cleansed call thou not unclean" (Acts 10:9-16).

Peter didn't understand the vision, but the Holy Spirit told him to go and talk to the three Gentiles who were inquiring about him downstairs. These Gentiles were sent from Cæsarea by a man named Cornelius. Cornelius was a Gentile, who had favor with God. Therefore, God sent an angel to him with a message. The angel instructed him to send for Peter, so Peter could preach the gospel to him.

After he spoke to these three men Peter understood what the vision meant. The next day Peter and three Jewish companions accompanied the Gentiles back to Cæsarea. When they arrived at Cornelius' house many guests had assembled there and were waiting for Peter. Peter began to preach the gospel, and all the Gentiles who heard the Word of God received the Holy Spirit just as the Jews did at the beginning (Acts 10:1-8, 17-48).

Soon after the Gentiles received the Holy Spirit, word reached to Jerusalem that Peter fellowshiped with the Gentiles. This was unlawful for any Jew to do. But, Peter defended himself before the counsel telling them that God had commanded him to do so. After listening to Peter, they realized that God had chosen out of the Gentiles a people for His name. Therefore, they held their peace and glorified God (Acts 11:1-18).

Introducing Paul the Apostle to the Gentiles

On the road to Damascus the Lord converted an infamous Pharisee named Saul. This man had formerly persecuted the Church, and was feared greatly by those who professed Christ as their Savior. In one encounter with Jesus Christ on the road to Damascus, Saul was converted and was later referred to as Paul. Paul grew in stature and authority, in the preaching of Jesus Christ as Lord and Savior (Acts 9:1-22).

Years later, Paul and Barnabas were preaching the great theme of justification by faith in a synagogue at Antioch. After the Jews had left the synagogue, the Gentiles sought Paul that he might preach these things to them on the next Sabbath day. When the next Sabbath day arrived, almost the whole city was gathered to hear Paul preach; as a result the Jews became very envious. While Paul was preaching they heckled and blasphemed him (Acts 13:42-45). Paul then turned to the Jews and said: "It was necessary that the word of God should first have been spoken unto you: but seeing ye put it from you, and judge yourselves unworthy of everlasting life, lo, we turn to the Gentiles" (Acts 13:46). This is an extremely important and pivotal moment in the ministry of the Apostle Paul. He officially acknowledged his calling as the Apostle to the Gentiles.

In Galatians 1:11 Paul gives us some very important information concerning the gospel that he preached to the Gentiles. "But I certify you, brethren, that the gospel which was preached of me is not after man. For I neither received it of man, neither was I taught it, but by the revelation of Jesus Christ" (Gal. 1:11-12).

Paul is clearly telling the Galatians and us, that he got his doctrine through revelations from Jesus Christ Himself. This was Paul's exclusive doctrine.

> But contrariwise, when they saw that the gospel of the uncircumcision was committed unto me, as the gospel of the circumcision was unto Peter; (for he that wrought effectually in Peter to the apostleship of the circumcision, the same was mighty in me toward the Gentiles:) . . . they gave to me and Barnabas the right hands of fellowship; that we should go unto the heathen [Gentiles], and they unto the circumcision. (Gal. 2:7-9)

Here Paul is claiming his apostleship is exclusively to the Gentile church, preaching a doctrine that he only received from Jesus.

At this point I would like to reiterate what Revelation 10:7 says: "But in the days of the voice of the seventh angel, when he shall begin to sound, the mystery of God should be finished, as he hath declared to his servants the prophets."

The fact that this mystery of God was declared to God's prophets means that this should be recorded in the Scriptures. We've already seen Joel's prophecy begin to be fulfilled on the day of Pentecost. The next question would then be, "Where else is it recorded what the prophets declared?"

The fact that God was going to save the Gentiles is well recorded. But, exactly how God was going to do it remained a mystery, until God commissioned Paul to be the apostle to the Gentiles. Through divine revelation, Jesus taught Paul the great doctrines concerning the Church that can only be found in the Pauline Epistles.

The Prophets Declared It

When the Apostle Paul was rejected by the Jews in Antioch he then turned to preaching to the Gentiles (Acts 13:46). Paul told the Jews that he got his orders from the Lord. Paul says, "For so hath the Lord commanded us, saying, 'I have set thee to be a light of the Gentiles, that thou shouldest be for salvation unto the ends of the earth.' " In this passage Paul was actually quoting from Isaiah 42:6. The prophet Isaiah said it this way:

> I the Lord have called thee in righteousness, and will hold thine hand, and will keep thee, and give thee for a covenant of the people, for a light of the Gentiles; To open the blind eyes, to bring out the prisoners from the prison, and them that sit in darkness out of the prison house. (Isa. 42:6-7)

Although Paul eventually became the apostle to the Gentiles, this prophecy's fulfillment began when Peter saw the vision of the unclean animals on the sheet (Acts 10:9-16). This fact was verified by the Apostle James to the council at Jerusalem (Acts 15:13-18). In Peter's defense, James quotes from Amos 9:11-12, who also prophesied about the salvation of the Gentiles. James boldly declared:

> And to this agree the words of the prophets; as it is written, After this I will return, and will build again the tabernacle of David, which is fallen down; and I will build again the ruins thereof, and I will

set it up: That the residue of men might seek after the Lord and all the Gentiles, upon whom my name is called, saith the Lord, who doeth all these things (Acts 15:15-17).

Thus, as the Lord spoke through the prophet Amos some eight hundred years prior to Peter's sermon at Cornelius' house, we can clearly see the prophetic record established in the Scriptures. Therefore, James used Amos' prophecy as the authority for Peter to preach the gospel to the Gentiles.

Although the prophets did prophesy about the salvation that would come to the Gentiles, theirs was only a declaration. However, how God would bring it to pass remained a mystery.

Of which salvation the prophets have inquired and searched diligently, who prophesied of the grace that should come unto you: Searching what, or what manner of time the Spirit of Christ which was in them did signify, when it testified beforehand the sufferings of Christ, and the glory that should follow. Unto whom it was revealed, that not unto themselves, but unto us [the apostles], they did minister the things which are now reported unto you [the church] by them that have preached the Gospel unto you with the Holy Ghost sent down from heaven: which things the angels desire to look into. (1 Pet. 1:10-12)

This astounding Scripture tells us that the prophets of old searched out diligently how and when the Lord would bring to pass the salvation that was not appointed for their time but for ours.

The Mystery Revealed

According to Paul's own testimony we know that he received his doctrine on the Church, by the direct revelation of Jesus Christ (Gal. 1:11-12). Although Jesus used Peter first, to preach the gospel to the Gentiles, it was

Paul who was appointed the Apostle to the Gentiles (Rom. 11:13). Paul declared that the Lord chose him *exclusively* to reveal the mystery through the gospel which Paul preached. Paul declares this truth in Romans 16:25-26.

> Now to him that is of power to stablish you according to my gospel, and the preaching of Jesus Christ, according to the revelation of the mystery, which was kept secret since the world began, But now is made manifest, and by the scriptures of the prophets according to the commandment of the everlasting God.

In this passage Paul tells us that the mystery that was hidden since the beginning of the world, was now made manifest through the Scriptures of the prophets, by the commandment of God. Remember this is what Paul told the Jews in Acts 13:47. He said that the Lord commanded him to preach to the Gentiles.

So, let's look at the revealing of the mystery that predates the world itself. In Ephesians 3:4-6, Paul writes:

> Whereby, when ye read, ye may understand my knowledge in the mystery of Christ. Which in other ages, was not made known unto the sons of men, as it is now revealed unto his holy apostles and prophets by the Spirit; That the Gentiles should be fellow heirs, and of the same body, and partakers of his promise in Christ by the gospel.

This mystery was that the Gentiles would be fellow heirs and partakers of the promises, forming a common body with Israel, by the gospel. The Lord placed the power of salvation in the preaching of the gospel, (Rom. 1:16; 1 Cor. 1:21; Luke 4:18). Therefore, through the gospel the Lord began constructing His Church, consisting of Jew and Gentile who together make up one Body (Eph. 2:14-18). Paul referred to the Jew and Gentile believers as a Body. The term *body* is defined by Paul in Ephesians 1:22-23. "And hath put all things under his feet, and gave him to be the head over all things to the church, Which is his body."

This is the Church that Jesus said He was going to build. But, the prophets of old only declared it. Although they diligently searched it out, the Lord raised up the Apostle Paul, to reveal the mystery. Paul became the only recorded apostle to whom Jesus revealed His mystery Body the Church.

This Body, the Church, started on the day of Pentecost and is still here today. It consists of all born again believers all around the world, whether living or dead. This is the Church that Jesus said He would return for and, *catch up* in the rapture. But, the rapture can only happen after the fullness of the Gentiles is come in—not a moment before. This leads us to the next phase of the mystery.

Continuing in the book of Ephesians, Paul adds another piece to the puzzle of the mystery church. "For we are members of his body, of his flesh, and of his bones. For this cause shall a man leave his father and mother and shall be joined to his wife, and they two shall be one flesh. This is a great mystery: but I speak of Christ and the church" (Eph. 5:30-32). The Apostle Paul calls this a great mystery. Not only are we members of Christ's Body, but the Church is also the Bride of Christ. We Christians who are Christ's Bride will be called to the marriage supper of the Lamb. A picture of heaven's greatest wedding day is found in Revelation. "Let us be glad and rejoice, and give honour to him: for the marriage of the Lamb is come, and his wife hath made herself ready. And he saith unto me, Write, Blessed are they which are called unto the marriage supper of the Lamb. And he saith unto me, These are the true sayings of God" (Rev. 19:7, 9).

Although John doesn't refer to the Bride as *the church*, like Paul does, we know this is in reference to the Church. Why? Because Paul tells us who the *bride* is in Ephesians. The revelation of the Body of Christ being the Bride of Christ was another element of the great mystery.

When the Apostle Peter was speaking of the prophets

that prophesied concerning the sufferings of Christ, he also mentioned the glory that would follow (1 Pet. 1:11). This is in reference to the final stage of the salvation process which is glorification. As the Apostle Paul told us in Romans 8:30, "Moreover whom he did predestinate, them he also called: and whom he called, them he also justified: and whom he justified, them he also glorified."

This will be actualized when the Lord returns for the Church, His Bride, in the rapture. At that time we will receive our glorified bodies which will be just like Jesus' glorious body. But, until that happens, Jesus has given us a hope of glory. In 1 John 3:2-3, we see the apostle speaking of the glorified bodies that we will receive at the appearing of Christ. Then he also says that every man who has this hope, purifies himself. Although we do not currently have our glorified bodies, Jesus has placed a down payment in us, forever claiming us for his Kingdom. This truth takes us to the next phase of the mystery.

In Colossians 1:25-27, Paul writes to this congregation concerning the fulfillment of the Word of God and the mystery.

> Whereof I am made a minister, according to the dispensation of God which is given to me for you, to fulfill the word of God. Even the mystery which hath been hid from ages and from generations, but now is made manifest to his saints: To whom God would make known what is the riches of the glory of this mystery among the Gentiles; which is Christ in you the hope of glory.

What a revelation! The outstanding feature of the Gentile church was the indwelling Holy Spirit that would abide with us and in us forever. Christ dwells in us today through the person of the Holy Spirit, who Himself is the seal and the earnest (down payment) of our inheritance (Eph. 1:13-14; John 14:16-27). This is our hope of the glory that will finally be manifested when Jesus takes away His beautiful Bride, the Church. As I stated before, Jesus'

Church will not be ready, until it reaches its fullness. When the last saints, whether living or dead, come into the Body of Christ (1 Cor. 12:13), then the Church will reach its fullness. Until that time Israel will remain in her state of blindness.

Israel's blindness is also a matter of prophetic record, according to Paul in Romans 11:7-10.

> What then? Israel hath not obtained that which he seeketh for; but the election hath obtained it, and the rest were blinded (According as it is written, God hath given them the spirit of slumber, eyes that they should not see, and ears that they should not hear;) unto this day. And David saith, Let their table be made a snare, and a trap, and a stumbling block, and a recompense unto them: Let their eyes be darkened, that they may not see, and bow down their back alway. (ref. Isa. 29:10; Ps. 69:22-23)

This is amazing; even Israel's blindness, which would have direct bearing on the Gentile church, was declared by the prophets. Although the church began on the day of Pentecost, and has been going on for over nineteen hundred years now, it will come to a sudden end when it reaches its fullness. This leads to the next phase of the mystery.

In 1 Corinthians 15:51-52, Paul tells us that the Church will leave this earth in the twinkling of an eye. "Behold I shew you a mystery; We shall not all sleep, but we shall all be changed, In a moment, in the twinkling of an eye, at the last trump: for the trumpet shall sound, and the dead shall be raised incorruptible, and we shall be changed." The rapture itself is the final phase of the mystery Body of Christ, the Church.

These are the elements of the mystery that we have covered thus far: (1) the mystery of Israel's blindness; (2) the mystery Body of Christ, the Gentile church; (3) The mystery Bride of Christ; (4) Christ in you, the mystery hope of glory. All of these mysteries are completed at the rapture of the Church, which is the final mystery. This rapture occurs at the last trumpet.

When we look at this from the perspective of Revelation 10:7, we can clearly see that God's mystery will also be completed at the sounding of the seventh trumpet. The only recurring theme of the word *mystery* in the New Testament is the mystery Church. Mystery is only found once in the Gospels (Mark 4:11), and in its plural form *mysteries* is only found twice (Matt. 13:11 and Luke 8:10). With the exception of the book of Revelation, the other uses of this word are only found in the Pauline Epistles.

Paul is basically the only apostle that writes concerning God's hidden mysteries. Why? Because he was chosen by Jesus Christ to reveal the mystery hidden since the beginning of the world. It was not revealed to any other person or generation, prior to the Apostle Paul. Clearly, Revelation 10:7 says it was declared or announced to the prophets of old; this fact is well documented. But, the mystery was revealed to Paul only.

The seventh trumpet is obviously the last one. According to the Apostle Paul, the mystery Church shall be completed at the last trumpet (1 Cor. 15:52). Hence, God's mysteries are completed at the sounding of the seventh or last trumpet.

When you look at the prophecy of the Old Testament, and the mention of the mystery Church in the New Testament, consider that the Church is the oldest mystery on record. Why? Because we (the Church) were all chosen in Christ before the world began (2 Tim. 1:9). The fact that Paul was chosen to reveal these truths, is seen in Acts 26:16–17, 19. Paul speaks of his initial encounter with Jesus. "But rise, and stand upon thy feet: for I have appeared unto thee for this purpose, to make thee a minister and a witness both of these things which thou hast seen, and of those things in the which I will appear [show] unto thee; Delivering thee from the people, and from the Gentiles, unto whom now I send thee; Where upon, O King Agrippa, I was not disobedient unto the heavenly vision."

To overlook Revelation 10:7, and give it some insignificant interpretation when all these Scriptures clearly back it up, is a crime. The pre-tribers miss these points and disregard many Scriptures for theological speculation. The mid-tribers also mistakenly say that the seventh trumpet happens in the middle of the week. Their basis is that the wrath of God starts in the middle of the seventieth week. Because the church is not appointed to wrath they conclude the seventh trumpet sounds in the middle of the week. Although this is close, it is not correct.

The important factor is when the beast takes away the daily sacrifice in the middle of the seventieth week, the wrath of God does not begin here. The wrath of God, as in the day of the Lord, can only come sometime after the abomination of desolation is set up. God's wrath will be in response to this final Gentile kingdom's ultimate blasphemy and abomination. The beast will have an unknown amount of time to make war with saints of the church and Israel's saved remnant. This time of calamities and satanic wrath will be interrupted by God's divine wrath. Then that which is determined [wrath] shall be poured out upon the desolator, the beast (Dan. 9:27).

Twelve

෨-෨ ෨-෨

The
Pre-Wrath Rapture Fact

In August 1993, while at the Milwaukee Rescue Mission, one of my students named Benito asked me, "So what are you, Pre-trib, Mid-trib?" I quickly responded, "I'm pre-wrath," which I might add is not a theory, but a biblical fact.

Unlike the Pre-trib theorist I do not consider the entire seventieth week of Daniel the day of the Lord, nor do I consider the entire seventieth week the wrath of God. The reason I do not make the pre-stated considerations is because the Bible doesn't make them. In 1 Thessalonians 5:9, the Apostle Paul tells us that we are not appointed to "wrath" (v. 9). Now if you use that verse alone, you can come up with many different conclusions as to what wrath is. However, Paul solves that problem for us because he makes that statement in reference to 1 Thessalonians 5:2, which clearly tells us that the "wrath" that Paul was speaking of is the "day of the Lord."

Within the context of the day of the Lord, this narrows down what one can call the wrath of God and remain within scriptural boundaries. From this point, I then use a system of themes from the Old Testament and align them with what Paul has told us in 1 Thessalonians, chapter 5. For example, Paul clearly links the day of the Lord with the wrath of God. This theme is consistent with Old Testament Scripture, as in Isaiah 13:9 and Zephaniah 1:14-15, 18.

The day of the Lord occurs after the abomination of desolation is set up. In 2 Thessalonians, chapter 2, Paul tells us that the day of the Lord can't happen until a "falling away" occurs and the man of sin is uncovered, the son of perdition (v. 3). He describes what is to be uncovered (v. 4), by giving us a picture of the abomination of desolation. This is when the uncovered beast walks into the temple of God declaring himself as God. According to Daniel, the beast begins his tyrannical rule with a blasphemous oratory (Dan. 7:8, 25; 11:36). However, he is only given three and one-half years to reign (Dan. 7:25). Revelation 13:5 says precisely the same thing. Because the breaking of the peace covenant happens in the middle of the seventieth week (Dan. 9:27), this is when the beast begins his forty-two month reign. This means that the abomination of desolation can only happen in the middle of the seventieth week of Daniel.

Jesus clearly states in Matthew 24:15, 21, when you see the abomination of desolation, "For then shall be great tribulation, such as was not since the beginning of the world to this time, no, nor ever shall be." In Mark 13:19-20, Jesus says the same thing. "For in those days shall be affliction, such as was not from the beginning of the creation which God created unto this time, neither shall be. And except that the Lord had shortened those days, no flesh should be saved."

The same theme (a time of trouble, such as never was since there was a nation even until the same time) is echoed in Daniel 12:1. In that passage the beast is already in power and the abomination of desolation is already in place. God's wrath commences on the beast and his kingdom in fulfillment of the prophecy found in Daniel 2. "His legs of iron, his feet part of iron and part of clay [the kingdom of the beast] Thou sawest till that a stone was cut out without hands, which smote the image upon his feet that were of iron and clay, and brake them to pieces" (Dan. 2:33-34).

The ten toes of this image represent the ten horns of Daniel 7:24 and Revelation 13:1. The wrath of God will strike the beast in the days of this ten-horned kingdom which is in the last half of the seventieth week. The wrath of God begins with first vial or bowl seen in Revelation 16:1-2.

The prophet Joel also alludes to this same theme in his prophecy "There hath not been ever the like, neither shall be any more after it, even to the years of many generations" (Joel 2:2). Here, Joel is speaking of the time period and one of the armies that will be mobilized. He identifies this period as the day of the Lord (Joel 2:1).

After the beast comes to power in the middle of the seventieth week, it takes him thirty days to set up the abomination of desolation, which totals 1,290 days (Dan. 12:11). The abomination of desolation will be a combination of the beast and the image of the beast entering into the Most Holy Place of the rebuilt Jewish temple (Matt. 24:15; Mark 13:14; Rev. 13:15-18; 2 Thess. 2:4).

At this point, I must reiterate that pre-trib theory uses exegetical arguments to back its teaching which states that the whole seventieth week is the wrath of God. However, the Bible narrows it down to *after* the middle of the seventieth week. There isn't one Scripture that says the day of the Lord begins prior to the beast becoming the beast. But, there are Scriptures that prove the day of the Lord comes after the abomination of desolation is in place. These Scriptures are Matthew 24:15, 21; Mark 13:14, 19; 2 Thessalonians 2:2-4; and Daniel 12:1.

Remember, he's only the beast for forty-two months, which begins in the middle of the seventieth week. Pre-tribers make the critical error of calling the man that will become the beast the beast at the beginning of the seventieth week. For example, it's like referring to George Washington's crossing the Delaware River during the Revolutionary War. Because we have the vantage point of hindsight, we know that the same person became the president of the United States. Therefore we may say, "Our first president crossed the Delaware." The fact is, although he crossed the Delaware, he wasn't in the role of the president when he did it. A similar analogy applies when we refer to the beast. Although the Scriptures pertaining to him are yet future, in a sense we have the vantage point of hindsight because God writes history in advance (Isa. 46:10). Therefore, many refer to the man of sin as the beast before his time; but that's wrong. He's not in that role until the middle of the seventieth week. Besides the man of sin cannot become the son of perdition until the beast is let out of the bottomless pit. Remember, he can only be revealed in his time (2 Thess. 2:6). There are no Scriptures that say we're not appointed to the seventieth week; instead, we are given the details of it, so we would know what shall befall us. The Bible says we're not appointed to the wrath of God. No other promises are made. Therefore, I agree with the Bible and disagree with the pre-trib position.

When it comes to the mid-trib position I agree that rapture occurs during the seventh trumpet, but I disagree that the seventh trumpet occurs exactly in the middle of the week. Remember the wrath of God will be in response to the beast's blasphemous activities. The abomination of desolation will be set up thirty days after the middle of the seventieth week. After the beast comes to power he will have an unknown amount of time to persecute and make war with the saints (Dan. 7:25; Rev.

13:7). But, his persecution of God's saints (the Church and Israel) will be interrupted by the outpouring of God's wrath. However before God's wrath begins, according to the prophet Joel and the Apostle Peter, cosmic disturbances will occur in the heavens (Joel 2:30–31; Acts 2:19–20). These cosmic disturbances will make it impossible to predict or calculate days with any accuracy. How long the cosmic signs are in the skies before the day of the Lord actually begins is unknown. Remember persecution, not the wrath of God, begins after the beast comes to power in the middle of the week (Rev. 13:7; Luke 21:11-12; 25-28). The rapture of the Church will occur at the seventh trumpet sometime after the abomination of desolation is in place, but before God pours out His wrath.

Much controversy has spawned out of the blowing of the seventh trumpet found in Revelation. As we saw in the last chapter, the seventh trumpet is one that is very important for the following reasons: (1) The mystery of God is completed. (2) The great announcement is made, "the kingdoms of this world are become the kingdoms of our Christ." (3) It is also the time of the dead where they shall be judged and receive their rewards. (4) It's the green light for commencement of God's wrath that takes place in the vial plagues. (5) Finally, the delay is terminated. Lets take a look at Revelation 11:18. "And the nations were angry, and thy wrath is come, and the time of the dead, that they should be judged, and that thou shouldest give reward unto thy servants the prophets, and to the saints, and them that fear thy name, small and great; and shouldest destroy them that destroy the earth."

A very interesting thing happens in this segment of the seventh trumpet. It's the time of reward for the dead; while at the same time, it's the time for commencement of wrath on the earth.

Let's consider the judgment of the dead first. Who are these dead? Are they sinners or saints? I think the text is very clear. They are obviously the righteous dead. These dead saints are resurrected in order to be rewarded.

Therefore this judgment (for reward) has to occur in Heaven. The roster of those attending this reward ceremony (the prophets, the saints and them that fear His name both small and great) tells us beyond the shadow of a doubt that this has to be the first resurrection. The pre-tribers say that this is not a resurrection. But, my question to them is how else can God reward dead people? What is He going to do, hang their rewards on their tombstones?

In the Gospel of John, Jesus tells us that there will be two distinct, general resurrections—the resurrection of the righteous unto the resurrection of life (eternal), and the resurrection of the unrighteous unto the resurrection of damnation (John 5:28-29). Jesus also tells us that these resurrections will include all that are in the graves. This passage of Scripture coincides with the "Church era" teaching that Paul received from Jesus. Paul declares this truth in his appeal before Felix in Acts 24:15. "And have hope toward God which they themselves also allow, that there shall be a resurrection of the dead, both of the just and unjust."

It is clear that this can only be the first resurrection as no mention of the unrighteous is seen here at all. Remember, God is rewarding dead saints.

The next thing that occurs during this segment of the seventh trumpet is the foreshadowing of God's wrath. Is it just coincidental that where wrath for the world is viewed, that reward for the saints is also in view? The fact that both are in view at the same time is actually consistent with the rest of the Scriptures. The simultaneous mention of both wrath and rapture can be seen in 2 Thessalonians 2:1-2. "Now I beseech you, brethren, by the coming of our Lord Jesus Christ, and by our gathering together unto him [rapture], That ye be not soon shaken in mind, or be troubled . . . as that the day of Christ [day of the Lord] is at hand."

I believe that Paul does this because there is a clear

scriptural relationship between the two. The same scenario is seen in Daniel 12:1-2.

> And at that time shall Michael stand up, the great prince which standeth for the children of thy people: and there shall be a time of trouble, such as never was since there was a nation even to that same time: and at that time thy people shall be delivered, every one that shall be found written in the book. And many of them that sleep in the dust of the earth shall awake, some to everlasting life and some to shame and everlasting contempt.

In these passages, both events are in view. As soon as the Lord takes the Church out of the world, His wrath can commence. This is why Paul identifies wrath with the day of the Lord in 1 Thessalonians 5. Paul is saying we're not appointed to WRATH. The prophets Isaiah and Zephaniah make the same association, as Paul does (Isa. 13:9; Zeph. 1:14-15).

Sound the Trumpet

As I already discussed, the seventh trumpet is also the completion of the mystery of God. Before God can return to get His Church, the fullness of the Gentiles must be reached (Rom. 11:25). When one considers that there are only two general resurrections (of life and of damnation), we can see why God waits for the numerical completion of the Church. When the Church reaches fullness then Israel can be released from her (mystery) blindness. Let's take a look at 1 Corinthians 15:51-52. "Behold I shew you a mystery; We shall not all sleep, but we shall all be changed, In a moment, in the twinkling of an eye, at the last trump: for the trumpet shall sound, and the dead shall be raised incorruptible, and we shall be changed."

In this passage Paul clearly infers that when the Church has reached its fullness, the Bride of Christ will be ready to attend the marriage supper of the Lamb. So the Church,

or the mystery Body of Christ now completed, is instantaneously changed, then caught up. This is the final phase
of the mystery; it occurs at the last trumpet.

At this point I must pose these facts and questions.
Fact: One of God's oldest secrets in the Scripture is the
mystery Church which is completed at the last trumpet
(Rom. 16:25; 1 Cor. 15:52). Question: Is it mere coincidence that Revelation 10:7 also says the mystery of God
will be completed at the sounding of the seventh (or last)
trumpet? Fact: Revelation 11:18 tells us that the judgment
of the righteous dead for reward is at the seventh trumpet. Question: Is it mere coincidence that the Church will
be raptured and receive her reward at the last trumpet?
(Rev. 22:12; Phil. 2:15-16; 1 Cor. 15:51-53). Fact: The
wrath of God commences on earth while reward for the
righteous dead is going on in heaven (Rev. 11:18). Question: Is it mere coincidence that the Church is also not
appointed to wrath and will be rewarded in heaven at the
last trumpet?

The evidence is clear. Especially since there is no
mention of the Church (supposedly) past Revelation 3,
until you get to Revelation 19. It's interesting that the
pre-tribers identify the Bride in Revelation 19 as the Body
of Christ. If it were not for Paul's letter to the Ephesians,
we wouldn't know that this was in reference to the Church.
Why? Because John doesn't call it the Church. However,
John does refer to the Church, in one of its elements of
mystery, as the "Bride of Christ."

The blowing of the last or seventh trumpet is another
element of the mystery Church. It's not a mere coincidence that resurrection and reward are seen in both 1
Corinthians 15 and Revelation 11:18. If pre-tribers used
the same interpretative logic that they used for the "Bride
of Christ" in Revelation 19, they would see that Revelation
11:18 also applies to the Church.

In 1 Thessalonians 4:15–17 we see the same scenario
as we did in 1 Corinthians, chapter 15.

For this we say unto you by the word of the Lord,

that we which are alive and remain unto the coming of the Lord shall not prevent them which are asleep. For the Lord himself shall descend from heaven with a shout, with the voice of the archangel, and with the trump of God: and the dead in Christ shall rise first: Then we which are alive and remain shall be caught up together with them in the clouds, to meet the Lord in the air: and so shall we ever be with the Lord.

In this passage we learn that the dead in Christ will rise first. As stated in 1 Thessalonians 4:15, we which are alive shall not "prevent" them which are asleep (dead). The word prevent, is translated from the Greek word *phthano* which means to proceed, or to go before hand. This verse states that the living will not precede the dead in the resurrection. When the last or seventh trumpet is sounded, the dead in Christ will rise first, then the living will be "caught up" to meet the Lord in the air.

The order of the resurrection is firmly established in 1 Corinthians 15:23. "But every man in his own order: Christ the first fruits, afterward they that are Christ's at his Coming." This passage clearly tells us that Jesus Himself was the first fruits, or the first one to raise from the dead in a glorified body. Then afterwards, "We that are His" will be raised at His coming. This passage does not give us any impression of a segmented rapture, nor of any multiple comings of the Lord.

The Bema Seat Judgment

In Revelation 11:18 where the seventh trumpet is concerned, one of the themes is reward of the saints (v. 18). Although this passage centers in on the dead being rewarded, from this we can clearly understand that it's a view of the "bema seat judgment." The dead can only be judged if they are first raised from the dead. According to Jesus (John 5:28-29) and Paul (Acts 24:15), there will only be two general resurrections, one for the righteous and one for the lost. Which one is viewed here? Obviously the first resurrection. It is this resurrection where the saints will be rewarded.

In 2 Corinthians 5:10, Paul tells us about this day of judgment. "For we must all appear before the judgment seat of Christ; that every one may receive the things done in his body, according to that he hath done, whether it be good or bad."

The word judgment in this passage comes from the Greek word, *bema*, which means judgment seat. This is where the saints will stand before Christ and give an account for their service to the Lord on earth. This will be a day where the secrets of Christian's hearts and motivations will be made manifest. Another more detailed account of this day of judgment can be found in 1 Corinthians 3:12–15.

> Now if any man build upon this foundation gold, silver, precious stones, wood, hay, stubble; Every man's work shall be made manifest: for the day shall declare it, because it shall be revealed by fire; and the fire shall try every man's work of what sort it is. If any man's work abide which he hath built thereupon, he shall receive a reward. If any man's work shall be burned, he shall suffer loss: but he himself shall be saved; yet so as by fire.

I believe after the Body of Christ is judged, then we will be ready to be offered up without spot nor wrinkle, unreproveable and unblamable (Col. 1:22; Eph. 5:27).

As I mentioned earlier, much of the book of Revelation is a kaleidoscope. There are places where Scriptures are fragmented into other themes. A good example of this is found in Revelation 20:4-5.

> And I saw thrones, and they sat upon them, and judgment was given unto them: and I saw the souls of them that were beheaded for the witness of Jesus, and for the word of God, and which had not worshiped the beast, neither his image, neither

had received his mark upon their foreheads, or in
their hands; and they lived and reigned with Christ
a thousand years. But the rest of the dead lived
not again until the thousand years were finished.
This is the first resurrection.

Here is where we see the rewards of the martyrs of
the tribulation period. These faithful saints are being
rewarded for their uncompromising commitment to Jesus,
which cost them their lives. We also learn that a period
of one thousand years separates the two resurrections.

Unfortunately, because this passage comes after Revelation 19, where the Lord returns, many say that this
reward scenario is also after the Lord returns. Again the
Scriptures don't say this; pre-tribers do. Just because this
passage is found in Revelation 20 does not mean that it's
occurring during the same time frame of the rest of that
passage. Much of the book of Revelation is not chrono-
logical. So therefore we must use the best rule for interpreting the Scriptures; and that is, "What do the rest of
the Scriptures on this subject say?"

Before I answer that question, let's put everything in
perspective. We know that the seventh trumpet blows and
the righteous dead are rewarded. We know that at the last
trumpet the Resurrection occurs. We know there are only
two general resurrections, separated by one thousand years
(John 5:28-29; Rev. 20:5). We know the saints are raptured in the first resurrection, before God's wrath kicks
in. Therefore, the reward ceremony in Revelation 20 is
actually a part of the Revelation 11:18 scenario. Why?
Because the Revelation 11:18 rewards scene is occurring
while the wrath of God is being poured out on the earth.
The scene in Revelation 20:4-6, also happens prior to the
wrath of God being poured out on the earth. How do I
know this? Let's take a look at Revelation 15:1-2.

And I saw another sign in heaven seven angels
having the seven last plagues; for in them is filled
up the wrath of God. And I saw as it were a sea

of glass mingled with fire: and them that had gotten the victory over the beast, and over his image and over his mark and over the number of his name, stand on a sea of glass, having the harps of God.

These saints are shown in heaven prior to the outpouring of the wrath of God. These saints were those who had gotten the victory over the beast, his mark, and his image. This means that the beast was already in power. This also means that this group of saints is the same as the saints in Revelation 13:7. The saints in Revelation 13:7 are the same saints that are seen in Revelation 20:4–6, because they are all identified by their refusal of the mark of the beast.

Because these saints are seen in heaven prior to the wrath of God, this is the same scenario that is seen in Revelation 11:18, where the dead saints were being rewarded, while wrath was beginning on the earth. These saints were called home at the blowing of the seventh or last trumpet just as the Church was. These were in heaven before wrath commenced on the earth, just as the Church is to be. These saints are part of the first resurrection, just as the Church is.

All these scenarios may appear to be different; but after close scrutiny of all the Scriptures, you can see that they are in fact the same, but from different kaleidoscopic angles.

Those Who Die in the Lord

In Revelation 14:13, we find an interesting statement made by the Holy Spirit. "And I heard a voice from heaven saying unto me Write, Blessed are the dead which die in the Lord from henceforth: Yea, saith the Spirit, that they may rest from their labors; and their works do follow them."

I think that it is very interesting that the Holy Spirit Himself makes this statement of comfort and assurance. It is a promise to all those who will die in the Lord, "hence-forth." What is meant by hence-forth? It means "from now on." There are two ways to interpret this Scripture. Either the Holy Spirit is speaking in relation to the time period of this passage, which is the future; or the Spirit is interjecting a church age truth, from John's perspective in A.D. 96.

It is the Holy Spirit's ministry to baptize the believers into the Body of Christ (1 Cor. 12:13); this is what makes us members of His Body. Paul used the phrase "in Christ" to teach us our relationship and position in Christ. Here the Holy Spirit is stating the same truth by making reference to those who "die in the Lord." As Paul says in Romans 6:5, "For if we have been planted together in the likeness of his death, we shall be also in the likeness of his resurrection." If this passage is to be interpreted from the futurists' viewpoint, there's a problem. If the Holy Spirit is to be taken from the earth during the tribulation then how are these saints going to die in the Lord? According to the Scriptures only the Holy Spirit can place you in Christ.

If the Holy Spirit is interjecting this truth here in this passage, then the Church is being mentioned in Revelation 14 contrary to pre-trib theory. Personally, I believe that the Holy Spirit is interjecting this statement of assurance because it applies to the entire church age including the time frame of this passage. The reason those who die in the Lord are blessed, is because the Lord shall return for those that are His at His coming (1 Cor. 15:23). At that time the dead in Christ will rise first (1 Thess. 4:15-16). Remember, according to the Scriptures there are only two general resurrections.

In Revelation 6:9–11, we see the souls under the altar. These are the souls of people who died in the Lord.

> And when he had opened the fifth seal, I saw under the altar the souls of them that were slain for the word of God, and for the testimony which they held: And they cried with a loud voice, saying How long, O Lord, holy and true, dost thou not

judge and avenge our blood on them that dwell on earth? And white robes were given to every one of them; and it was said unto them, that they should rest yet for a little season, until their fellowservants also and their brethren, that should be killed as they were, should be fulfilled.

This Scripture is absolutely amazing. The Lord in His omniscience knows exactly who are His, and exactly how many of them there are. This is why He told these souls to wait for a season, until the number of their brethren, who will be killed like they were, is filled up. Filled up means numerically complete. This scene is obviously prior to the wrath of God, as the Lord hadn't returned to the earth to avenge them yet.

Since the dead in Christ must rise first, the Lord must wait for their number to be completed. Therefore, He told these martyred saints to wait for the rest of their brethren that must also die as they did. This would coincide with waiting for the fullness of the Gentiles to come in. In the next verse, the opening of the sixth seal is the vision of the wrath of God. This would logically follow the numerical completion of the total number of dead in Christ, prior to the wrath of God being poured out. This passage of Scripture adheres to the same theme as the other Scriptures that we've covered. In each case God's elect are off the earth prior to the outpouring of His wrath.

One thing that I want to stress again is that everything I've presented so far has been all Scripture and no theology. I have maintained consistency in the Scriptures as the rule of thumb for interpretation. I don't stretch the Bible to make it say what it doesn't actually say.

Thirteen
ๆๆ ๆๆ

Why They
Can't See the Church

One of the most common arguments used to defend the pre-trib doctrine is, "The Church is not mentioned in the book of Revelation from the end of chapter three up until chapter nineteen. Since the 'Church' is not mentioned, between these chapters, that means nothing between Revelation 4:1 and 19:7-9 can possibly pertain to the Body of Christ." They say that the entire church age is pictured in Jesus' address to the seven churches of Asia Minor (Rev. 2 and 3).

From the pre-trib view, the church age is to close out in the Laodicean state, which is synonymous with apostasy. After Revelation 3, they then reference Revelation 4:1 as a picture of the rapture. "After this I looked, and behold, a door was opened in heaven: and the first voice which I heard was as it were a trumpet talking to me;

which said, Come up hither, and I will shew thee things which must be hereafter."

As one of the popular commentaries puts it, this seems to be the fulfillment of 1 Thessalonians 4:14-17 (the rapture).

This is stretching what the Scriptures say. To get that interpretation from this verse you have to read a great deal into this passage. In 1 Thessalonians 4:14–17, no opening of any door in heaven is mentioned. The passage clearly says that the Lord Himself shall descend from heaven, and the Church will meet Jesus in the clouds. This is a perfect example of making the Scriptures say something that is simply not there.

First of all, when has the "body of John" been a type of "Body of Christ?" When has John the Apostle been a type of the Church? Although other biblical characters have been likened unto the Church, show me one Scripture that suggests in the slightest way that John is a type of the Church. John himself never claimed to be such. Nor is it stated in any way or found in any Scripture, in the Old or New Testaments. There is absolutely no scriptural authority to back up this interpretation.

The seven churches that were addressed were seven actual, local congregations in their respective cities of Asia Minor. All of these churches had areas of strength and weakness where the Lord praised them or rebuked them.

The moral and ethical problems these churches faced are not exclusively intrinsic of just these ancient congregations. The reason is people, in general, do not change. Man's sinful nature has been a constant since the Fall of Adam. Therefore, the admonitions and rebukes the Lord gives to these churches can find application in any church age. This is why the Spirit states, "Those that have an ear let them hear what the Spirit says to the churches."

In the book of Revelation, the word *church* is found seven times. In each use, it is in reference to a local congregation. For example, in Revelation 2:1 it says, "unto the angel of the church of Ephesus." Church here is in reference to that particular congregation. The word *churches* is used thirteen times. An example of how it's used can be found in Revelation 3:13, "He that hath an ear let him hear what the Spirit says unto the churches." Again this is local; it infers local congregation(s). In the book of Revelation, whether singular or plural, the use of the word "Church" is certainly local in application.

Since pre-trib theory tells us that much of the book of Revelation doesn't apply to the Church, the logical question is, "Then to whom does it apply? In Revelation 10:10, we are given some information on to whom John's prophecy was written. "And I took the little book out of the angel's hand, and ate it up; and it was in my mouth sweet as honey: and as soon as I had eaten it, my belly was bitter. And he said unto me, Thou must prophesy again before many peoples, and nations, and tongues, and kings."

At the time John wrote the book of Revelation, it was approximately A.D. 96. By this time John was an old man, the last of the original twelve apostles who was still alive. Being banished to the island of Patmos by Emperor Domitian of Rome, he was instructed to write down the visions contained in this book. After being banished to this island, it was highly unlikely that John would be going on a worldwide evangelical tour. Yet, the angel told him that "he" must prophesy before the nations, peoples and tongues. The only possible way for John to give this prophecy to the peoples, nations, and tongues was to write this vision in a book. According to many authorities the book of Revelation became generally accepted some time in the third century. However, from the "futurist" perspective this book is highly prophetic, with many things yet remaining to be fulfilled.

If the first three chapters of this prophecy addressed to seven churches in Asia Minor represent the entire church age, then to whom is the rest of the book of the Revelation written to? Well, certainly the angel told John to prophesy to the nations, peoples, tongues and kings.

Can anyone deny that this has been in fulfillment for centuries now? When the Bible speaks of the nations and peoples, unless Israel is specifically named, this applies to Gentiles. Without a doubt, the book of Revelation was written to and for Christians. If this were not the case, do you think it would be in the Christian Bible? The fact that the Christians have had it in their Bible for centuries is a fulfillment of what the angel told John, "Prophesy again unto the nations, people and tongues."

John had already written three Epistles and had done much work with Peter. According to the angel in Revelation 19:10, "the testimony of Jesus is the spirit of prophecy." That statement is directed to the Gentile Church. Who else has had the testimony of Jesus for the last two thousand years? Certainly, the Church has been blessed from reading and hearing the prophecies of this book (Rev.1:3).

Why didn't the angel simply tell John to prophesy to the Body of Christ? Why doesn't John use the word *church*, beyond its local meaning, like the Apostle Paul uses it? The answer is simple. The revelation of the Church as the Body of Christ was only given to the Apostle Paul. Paul didn't write the book of Revelation, John did. Therefore, you will not find John referring to all born-again believers as the Church. You simply cannot look through the eyes of Pauline doctrine, and expect to see the Church in John's writings. John didn't go to Dallas Theological Seminary to learn Pauline theology, nor is there any evidence that John was a student of Paul.

Paul tells us in his Epistles that the revelation of the mystery Church which was hidden for ages, was revealed to him exclusively. In Romans 16:25, Paul calls the revelation of this mystery, "my gospel." Paul proclaims the same truth in Galatians 1:11–12. "The gospel which was preached of me is not after man, for I neither received it of man, neither was I taught it, but by the revelation of Jesus Christ." It is clear that the gospel that Paul preached was committed to him, not John.

In the Epistles of John and in the book of Revelation, John never uses the word *church* in other than a local sense. John never uses the word *church*, in the way Paul uses it, such as the Church as the Body of Christ. The only time the word *church* is found, other than in the book of Revelation, is in Third John.

The Epistle of Third John is addressed to an unknown church that was being dominated by a man named Diotrephes. In the text of this short Epistle, the use of the word *church* is local. In the Gospel of John the word is not used at all.

Not only in John's Epistles are the terms *Body of Christ* and *church*, in the sense of the mystery Church, not found, but it is equally absent in the other Epistles. The word *church* is only used twice in the other Epistles. In both cases, *church* is used in a local sense (ref. 1 Pet. 5:13 and James 5:14). Pauline theology cannot be found in any other New Testament author's vocabulary. It simply isn't there. One must keep in mind that John, not Paul, wrote the book of Revelation; therefore, you will not find Pauline vernacular.

So how does one see the Church in the book of Revelation? First of all, one has to realize that those who say it's not mentioned between Revelation 3 and 19 can't see it because their theory says it's not there. It is there, but pre-trib theory says, "It can't be," so therefore they don't and won't see it. It's like a search team looking for a lost item. If the person in charge of this search team looks in a certain place and doesn't find the lost item, he tells the others, "I've thoroughly searched this room and the item is not in here." He may give several reasons to back up his findings. He may say, "I looked everywhere; under the table, in the closet, etc." Because he's the boss, his word has validity. From that point on, the word on that room he searched is, "It isn't in there." What if the boss is wrong? Everyone that goes by his assessment has made the same mistake the boss has made.

Not long ago, I was listening to one of my favorite radio ministers, Chuck Swindoll, on a local Christian station in Milwaukee. Pastor Swindoll made a very candid and honest statement; he said, "I'm pre-trib, but what if Jesus isn't?" Pastor Swindoll was in no way renouncing his pre-trib position, but he was saying, "What if the way we look at certain things in the Bible is wrong? What if some of our theologies need to be re-evaluated?"

Much of what we believe in Christianity is what the authorities or the books say. Like the scenario I used above, the words of the pre-trib authorities and publications are like the boss who says, "It isn't in there." Thus, many that read the book of Revelation believe as all the others do, "The Church isn't in there." Consequently, by the time the Bible student gets to the book of the Revelation, he is already pre-disposed not to see the Church. Moreover, any passage found in the book of Revelation that refers to the Church is painstakingly explained away and is given some frivolous interpretation. Pre-trib theory has a serious weakness here because they usually don't have any solid Scriptures to back up their reasoning. At that point they switch from the Scriptures to exegetical arguments.

The Blinders Off

The first step in getting someone to see the Church in the book of Revelation is to remove the pre-trib blinders. Pre-trib doctrine pre-disposes people not to see the Church by a process of bad interpretations of some key Scriptures. If one will re-evaluate the Scriptures that I will list and stop using pre-trib theories to interpret them, you will be in position to see the Church in Revelation.

First, stop calling the "he" and the "what" of 2 Thessalonians, chapter 2, the Holy Spirit. I know the reason that this interpretation has remained for so long. Remember, the authorities reach this conclusion based on the question, "Who else can it be?" Because the word *he* is used, they refer to Jesus' statements in John 14-16, which is logical if there is no one else to consider. However, Paul does not say the *he* is the Holy Spirit. Because few have acknowledged the tri-part reality of the beast and believe that Satan possesses the Anti-christ, Revelation 17:8 has been badly interpreted and overlooked. The demonic aspect of the beast is in the bottomless pit. Unless the angel who has the responsibility to lock and unlock the bottomless pit opens it and lets the demon loose, the beast can't ascend out of the bottomless pit. Therefore, he cannot possess his human counterpart, "the son of perdition." Also remember that angels are always referred to in the masculine, and we don't know their names other than what the Scriptures reveal. This passage in 2 Thessalonians is the "flagship" Scripture of pre-trib doctrine and seems to support their theory the best. But, once you see that the *he* and *what* are not the Holy Spirit, a critical blow is dealt to this theory.

Second, stop interpreting the word *revealed*, found in 2 Thessalonians 2:3, as the initial appearance or the coming of the beast. The Greek word used in this text is *apokalupto* which is translated to mean "to uncover." It does not mean the first time you see someone in a particular arena or setting. You can know someone for years, and yet they could have an unknown characteristic uncovered tomorrow.

When it is interpreted as identify, initial appearance, or his coming, it gives people the impression of the beginning of the seventieth week when the man of sin signs the covenant. That's wrong. Besides, he's not even the beast then; he's only the beast for the last half of the seventieth week, forty-two months. Disregard theology; rely on what the Bible says.

Third, stop going by theological conclusions about what the wrath of God is and when it begins. Look to what Scriptures identify as the wrath of God. One won't go wrong if one looks at it as Paul does in 1 Thessalonians, chapter 5. In that text the wrath of God occurs during the day of the Lord. Paul says that the day of the Lord can't happen until the abomination of desolation occurs (ref. 2 Thess. 2:3-4).

In Revelation, chapter 5, concerning Christ's opening of the seals, His authority to do so is the object of the text, not His wrath. Besides that, the sixth seal is just the kaleidoscopic vision of the wrath of God that will actually be poured out in the vials of Revelation 16. The wrath of God does not begin at that point. How can "that determined" (wrath, ref. Dan. 9:27) be poured out on the beast before he even becomes the beast? He's only the beast for forty-two months, the last half of the seventieth week. At the beginning of the week, he's the rider on the white horse not yet uncovered as the beast. As Daniel tells us, "In the days of these kings (ten toes/ten horns) shall the God of heaven set up a kingdom, which shall never be destroyed . . . but it shall break into pieces and consume all these kingdoms" (Dan. 2:44).

This is why Paul told the Thessalonians that day (the day of the Lord) shall not come until the uncovering of the son of perdition occurs. He then gives us a description of the abomination of desolation to show us what the beast will do once he's uncovered. This lines up with what Jesus said, "When ye therefore shall see the abomination of desolation . . . stand in the holy place" for then there shall be tribulation as was not since the beginning of the world" (the day of the Lord) (Matt. 24:15, 21).

Fourth, stop giving the Holy Spirit the restraining ministry. There is not one Scripture that actually says that. The closest one is found in Isaiah 59:19. However, that passage is in reference to the Spirit lifting up the Redeemer. Jesus Christ Himself is the standard. Pre-trib interpretation of this passage as a proof text for the restrainer of 2 Thessalonians is purely theological, and based on the assumption that Paul was referring to the Holy Spirit. I'm not saying that the Holy Spirit can't or doesn't restrain evil. I am saying that building entire theories around an assumption needs to be reconsidered. Angels restrain demonic spirits according to the Scriptures. The Holy Spirit is God, and God has angels to handle fallen angels. In His sovereignty God does set boundaries, but

the literal restraint of demons is handled by His angels.
Pre-trib theory also has the Holy Spirit leaving the earth,
during the seventieth week. There is not one Scripture
that says that either. Remember neither the Bible nor
Paul says that; pre-trib theory does.

Fifth, stop looking through the eyes of Pauline theology to see the Church in the book of Revelation. Paul
didn't write the book of Revelation; John did. Of course,
John doesn't use terms like Body of Christ or the Church
to mean all born-again believers. Those terms can only be
found in the writings of Paul.

If they would just use the same logic that they used
to determine the identity of the Church in Revelation 19,
there would be less confusion. John doesn't mention the
Church in that passage, but he does say, "The Bride." It's
only through Pauline theology that we know John is referring to the Church. If they used the same interpretive
logic in Revelation 11:15-18, they would see the Church
there also. However, that would cause serious problems
for pre-trib theory.

If one can get over these theoretical hurdles, one is
in a much better position to see the Church in the book
of Revelation.

The Judgment Seat

In Revelation 20:4-6, we see the judgment of the
saints that were slain during the reign of the beast. Contained in these verses is some important information
concerning these saints.

> And I saw thrones, and they that sat upon them,
> and judgment was given to them: and I saw the
> souls of them that were beheaded for the witness
> of Jesus, and for the word of God, and which had
> not worshipped the beast, neither his image, nei-
> ther had received his mark upon their foreheads,
> or in their hands; And they lived and reigned with
> Christ a thousand years. But the rest of the dead
> lived not again until the thousand years were fin-

ished. This is the first resurrection. Blessed and holy is he that hath part in the first resurrection: on such the second death hath no power, but they shall be priests of God and of his Christ, and shall reign with Him a thousand years.

What I would like to do at this point is to compare these saints and the Church saints.

Saints: These were killed for the testimony of Jesus, and for "The word of God" (v. 4).

Church saints: The Apostle John was definitely a Christian, but John didn't call himself one; nor did he say he was in Christ. In Revelation 1:9, John stated that he was banished to the island of Patmos for the Word of God and the testimony of Jesus. This is the same reason why the saints of Revelation 20 were martyred. Now wouldn't it be an error to say John wasn't a "Church saint" or a Christian simply because he doesn't call himself one, or mention the Church?

Saints: These saints are witnesses of Jesus (v. 4).

Church saints: The Church saints are witnesses of Jesus. The only way to become a true witness of Jesus is by being born of the Spirit, and Holy Ghost filled (Acts 1:8).

Saints: These saints held fast to the Word of God, and are being rewarded (vv. 4-6).

Church saints: The Church holds fast to the Word of God.

> For it is God which worketh in you both to will and to do of his good pleasure. Do all things without murmurings and disputings: That ye may be blameless and harmless, the sons of God, without rebuke, in the midst of a crooked and perverse nation, among whom ye shine as lights in the world; Holding forth the word of life; that I may rejoice in the day of Christ [day of reward]. . . . (Phil. 2:13-16)

Saints: These saints will reign with Christ (v. 4).

Church saints: The Church was promised to reign with Christ (2 Tim. 2:12; Rev. 2:26-27; 5:9-10).

Saints: These saints are blessed and holy (v. 6).

Church saints: The Church saints are the Lord's blessed and are also holy (Eph. 1:3; James 1:12; 1 Pet. 1:16, 2:9; Col. 1:22).

Saints: These saints are in the first resurrection (v. 5).

Church saints: The Church is in the first resurrection (John 5:29; 1 Cor. 15:23, 51-52; 1 Thess. 4:15-17).

Saints: These are called "saints" (Rev. 13:8).

Church saints: The Church members of the Body of Christ are called "saints," and are sanctified (1 Cor. 6:11; 2 Tim. 2:21; Heb. 2:11, 10:10-14).

Saints: These are called the "priests of God" (v. 6).

Church saints: The Church is called a royal priesthood (1 Pet. 2:9).

Saints: These were faithful unto death (v. 4).

Church saints: The Church is commanded to be faithful unto death (Rev. 2:10; Luke 9:24; Matt. 24:13; Ps. 116:15).

Saints: These have their names written in the Lamb's book of life from the foundation of the world (Rev. 13:8).

Church saints: The Church has their names written in the Lamb's book of life and are chosen in Christ from the foundation of the world (2 Tim. 1:9).

Saints: These are delivered from the second death (v. 6).

Church saints: The Church is promised to be delivered from the second death (Rev. 2:10-11).

Saints: Those who got the victory over the mark of the beast were not appointed to the wrath of God (Rev. 15:1-2).

Church saints: The Church was promised not to have to endure the wrath of God (1 Thess. 5:2, 9).

Saints: These saints are said to be Gentiles (Rev. 7:9).

Church saints: The Church is the Gentile church.

Saints: These saints are washed in the blood of the Lamb (Rev. 7:14).

Church saints: The Church is washed in the blood of the Lamb (Eph. 1:7; Col. 1:14; 1 John 1:7).

Saints: These saints have a resurrection and rewards ceremony at the seventh or last trumpet while wrath is being poured out on the earth (Rev. 11:18; 20:4; 15:1-2).

Church saints: The Church is raised at the last trumpet and is rewarded while wrath is being poured out on the earth (1 Cor. 15:51-53; Rev. 22:12; 1 Thess. 4:15-17; 5:2, 9).

Are all fifteen of these matches just mere coincidence? I know someone will come up with the argument, "Well, you can come up with a thousand matches between a Chinese and an African, but they are two different types of people." Although that's true, the fact is these comparisons aren't my only basis of argument. When you consider all of the other evidence I have already given you in this book, these comparisons are just icing on the cake. The so-called tribulation saints are actually the last generation of Church saints.

With the pre-trib blinders off, consider what the Bible says. There are two general resurrections which will include all that are in the graves. These two resurrections are separated by one thousand years. The so-called tribulation saints are part of the first resurrection. They have to go up exactly when the Church does, or you are forced to say that they are raised at the end of the seventieth week of Daniel. If this is your position, you have no Scriptures to prove that; that's a theological argument.

Revelation 15:1-2 shows the tribulation saints in heaven before the wrath of God even starts. Thus, the tribulation saints couldn't be raised at the end of the seventieth week. You cannot prove that the rapture has two separate segments for two general groups in the same first resurrection. To prove that point you must leave what the Scriptures say and interject pre-trib theology.

The split first resurrection argument seems to be feasible to pre-tribers simply because the passage is found in Revelation 20. They contend that in this chapter Christ has already returned to the earth; therefore, this scene has to be at the end of the seventieth week. However, there is a problem created by the segmented rapture theory. According to 1 Thessalonians 4:15, "We which are alive and remain unto the coming of the Lord shall not prevent [precede] them which are asleep."

If what Paul tells us in 1 Corinthians 15:23 is true, then "those that are Christ's" (which includes the tribulation saints) will be changed in a twinkling of an eye, at His coming. When Christ comes He will come in the clouds, accompanied by His angels, and the trumpet shall sound, and the dead in Christ shall rise first. This is the first resurrection (remember there are only two general resurrections: the just and the unjust).

If the first resurrection occurs prior to the seventieth week, and then another resurrection of the dead occurs seven years later, then the living will precede the dead. Here's the scenario: The dead in Christ are raised first, and the living caught up, all before the seventieth week begins. The problem with placing another resurrection at the end of the seventieth week is that you would have a group of resurrected dead raptured before the beginning of the seventieth week, and another group of resurrected dead at the end of the seventieth week. The saints who were alive and raptured at the beginning of the seventieth week would precede the dead that are raised at the end of the seventieth week by seven years. Paul clearly states that the Lord said the living would not precede the dead in Christ. However, in the pre-trib theory that's exactly what happens, the living do precede the dead.

Another problem that is created by the pre-trib doctrine is, according to Revelation 20:5, after the first resurrection the rest of the dead do not live again until a thousand years are completed. If the pre-tribers have it their way, the Scriptures would be wrong again. According to their theory, the first resurrection occurs prior to the seventieth week. But, since the Lord is in some big hurry, He leaves the rest of the saints, and returns seven years later (not one thousand years), to raise the others He'd left behind. The pre-trib response to that is, "All of the resurrections prior to the resurrection of damnation are first, in a sense. But, Jesus didn't say it in that sense." That reasoning is not valid.

First of all, it was Jesus who said there would be two general resurrections; and He knew all about Enoch, Elijah, and the two witnesses of Revelation, chapter 12, when He said it. If the Lord decides to do something outside the realm of the two general resurrections, that's His business. He's God; He can do that. One cannot use Elijah and Enoch to prove that the first resurrection is split into two groups separated by seven years. There simply are no Scriptures to prove that.

The Innumerable Multitude

In Revelation 7, we see an innumerable multitude of people in heaven and 144,000 saints of the twelve tribes of Israel on earth.

> After this I beheld, and lo, a great multitude, which no man could number, of all nations, and kindreds, and people, and tongues, stood before the throne, and before the Lamb, clothed with white robes, and had palms in their hands; And one of the elders answered, saying unto me, What are these which are arrayed in white robes? and whence came they? And I said unto him, Sir, thou knowest. And he said unto me, These are they which came out of great tribulation, and have washed their robes, and made them white in the blood of the Lamb. (Rev. 7:9, 13-14)

Before I begin to comment on this magnificent multitude, we must first understand who they are not. These are not the survivors of the wrath of God who remain on earth in their natural bodies. Why do I say this? Because these are seen in heaven (Rev. 7:9). Undoubtedly, there will be millions of Gentiles left on earth who will go right into the millennium in their natural bodies. So, I don't want you to get them confused. These are not the children of Israel. Israel's remnant will also go right into the millennial kingdom, in their natural bodies. Finally, according to the pre-trib authorities, this is a multitude of Gentiles; but it's not the Church.

Let's look at who this multitude is. First of all because they are from the nations, tongues, and peoples, I would agree that these are indeed Gentiles. Since they are out of the great tribulation, that means they were living during the reign of the beast. This would certainly imply that they are on earth past the middle of the seventieth week. However, they are seen in heaven before the throne of God. They are in heaven, while the 144,000 of Israel are on earth. If (according to pre-trib theory) they are not the Church Gentiles, and they can't be the Gentiles who remain on earth and go into the millennium; yet, they are so many that they were beyond numbering, from every nation, tongue and people; then who could they possibly be?

Let's look at some more clues. Because they are "out of the great tribulation," one would have to put these in the same time frame as the tribulation saints of Revelation 15 and 20. These saints of those chapters are clearly identified as "tribulation saints," because they refused to get the mark of the beast. It is clear that the tribulation saints in Revelation 15, are in heaven prior to the outpouring of the wrath of God. The fact that these three groups of saints (Rev. 7, 15 and 20) are all linked to the tribulation period, means all three are the same era of Gentiles.

This same era of Gentiles, according to Revelation, chapter 20, are in the first resurrection. This is why I believe they are seen in heaven. Because there is no Scriptural authority to split the first resurrection into two separate groups, then as the Scriptures say in 1 Corinthians 15:23, Christ comes back for all those that are His at His coming.

The Bible has no account of another multitude of

Gentiles, from every nation, people, and tongue, who are also in the first resurrection, but not part of the Church. From the day of Pentecost to the first resurrection is the age of the Gentile Church. The only other group of Gentiles are those left of the nations that go into the millennial kingdom in their "natural bodies." If the Gentiles of Revelation 7 are not the Church, then where do they come from, and how do they get to heaven? Is there a third resurrection that transports them into heaven?

Remember, the sixth seal has the vision of wrath in it. Everywhere the identified (not speculated) wrath of God is mentioned, Gentiles are seen in heaven. For example, during the sixth seal, wrath on earth is "visioned," while the Gentiles are in heaven. Israel is on earth (Rev. 6:12-17; 7).

Also in Revelation 11:18, wrath is on earth after the "Great Announcement" is made; the dead are resurrected and are being rewarded in heaven at the seventh (last) trumpet.

Moreover in Revelation 15:1-2, tribulation saints are in heaven prior to wrath on earth.

Remember (1) Tribulation saints are Gentiles, as is the church. (2) Tribulation saints are not appointed to the wrath of God (Rev. 15:1-2). Neither is the church (1 Thess. 5:2, 9). (3) The tribulation saints are resurrected and rewarded at the seventh or last trumpet (Rev. 11:18). So is the Church (1 Cor. 15:51-53).

The Fullness of the Gentiles

Although the pre-trib theory paints pretty pictures, it's hard to prove. They say that the Church is gone from the earth and misses all the suffering. They'll just be caught right up into heaven before any of the trouble starts in the seventieth week and live in heavenly bliss for eternity. According to the pre-tribers, the Gentiles of the tribulation period will be resurrected at the end of the tribulation, but the Church will be gone at least seven years prior to that. That all sounds fine, but it's not scripturally sound.

The reason I say this is because Israel cannot be released from her state of national and spiritual blindness until the fullness of the Gentiles is come in. One thing that not even the pre-tribers can deny is that the tribulation saints are Gentiles, as is the Church. How is it that Jesus does not wait until the "full number of Gentiles" comes in before the first resurrection takes place? That he has to come back seven years later, (according to the pre-tribers) to get the rest of the Gentiles, implies that Jesus does not wait for the fullness of the Gentiles. Doesn't 1 Corinthians 15:23 tell us that, "they that are Christ's at His coming" include Revelation 7 Gentiles?

In Romans 11:25, the Lord, through Paul, accurately states "fullness of the Gentiles," not "completion of the Church." The fullness of the Gentiles implies the completion of the church, but that's not the emphasis of the mystery in this passage. The emphasis is completion or fullness of the Gentiles. How could Jesus fulfill that aspect of the mystery when He leaves an innumerable multitude of Gentiles behind? When the fullness of the Gentiles is reached, then Israel will be released from her national blindness. She will recognize and submit to the Lordship of Jesus Christ as the King of kings and Lord of lords. Israelites will also come into total knowledge of their ethnic identity.

Since Israel has been in dispersion all over the earth for centuries, it would be impossible to simply look at one's skin and tell who is from which of the twelve tribes. Even in John's day there were those who said they were Jews and were not (Rev. 2:9, 3:9). After the fullness of the Gentiles is come in and Israel is released from blindness, the angel will seal twelve thousand from each tribe. Can you imagine it? There will not be just three or four witnesses, but twelve thousand, of each tribe. There are going to be some big surprises because God knows the blood lines.

What we see in Revelation 7 is the Gentiles in fullness in heaven, while the 144,000 are on the earth. What John is looking at are future Christians of the last Church generation who are washed in the blood of the Lamb. This will occur right before the wrath of God begins. In the book of Acts, Peter's sermon on the day of Pentecost astonished the Jews who had come to Jerusalem. Although many mocked the movement of the Holy Spirit, Peter stood up with boldness and declared to them that this was the fulfillment of the prophecy of Joel. "And it shall come to pass in the last days, saith God, I will pour out of my Spirit upon all flesh: . . . (Acts 2:17). This was the beginning of the Church that Jesus said He was going to build. Peter also tells us when the church age will end in Acts 2:20. "The sun shall be turned into darkness, and the moon into blood, before that great and notable day of the Lord come."

Notice the familiar theme of the cosmic disturbances happens before the day of the Lord comes. This is why Paul was careful to tell us that we are not appointed to the wrath of God that occurs during the day of the Lord (1 Thess. 5:2, 9). In Peter's sermon we are given the beginning and the end of the entire church age, from Pentecost to before the day of the Lord comes.

Now there are some that claim *before* in this passage doesn't really mean before. This is ridiculous. It is a perfect example of making the revelation of God's truth subordinate to the grammatical rules of men's language and academia. Paul warned us against this in 1 Timothy 6:4. "He is proud, knowing nothing, but doting about questions and strifes of words, whereof cometh envy, strife, railings, evil surmisings."

In this passage *words* is translated from the Greek word *logomachia*, where we get our English word *logomachy*, which means, "A contention or debate marked by the reckless or incorrect use of words." This is why Paul (a scholar) when addressing the Corinthians said that he didn't come with the wisdom of men's words, or with excellency of speech, or enticing words of men's wisdom, but in the demonstration of the Spirit and power, that their faith wouldn't stand in the wisdom of men, but in the power of God.

Paul continues to say that we have not received the spirit of the world, but the Spirit of God, that we might know the things freely given unto us of God (1 Cor. 1 and 2). It is the ministry of the Holy Spirit to teach us, and to show us things to come (John 16:13). Grammatical rules and structure are useful and needed, but they should never be the substance of interpretation alone. Some of us adhere to the tenets of Greek and Hebrew grammar more than the illumination of the Holy Spirit causing simple things to become difficult and confusing. We break passages and words down so far until they lose their meaning. We have wandered far when words like before don't really mean before at all.

Thus we see Israel's tribulation ministry on earth, the Gentiles in heaven, and the wrath of God, all during the sixth seal. It's not possible that Jesus would fail to wait for the fullness of the Gentiles to come in, only to return to the earth at least seven years later to get another multitude of Gentiles. Either He waits for their fullness or He doesn't wait. The tribulation saints cannot be raised at the end of the tribulation, as pre-trib doctrine suggests. They are raised and rewarded at the last trumpet (Rev. 11:18). They were not appointed to the wrath of God because they are in heaven before the wrath of God begins (Rev. 15:1-2). They are saints who are washed in the blood of Jesus Christ (Rev. 7:14). The Lord knows those that belong to Him, and He shall rapture all of them that are His at His coming.

Fourteen

❧❧ ❧❧

Babylon

In the first chapter we discussed King Nebuchadnezzar's dream. In his dream the Lord foretold the succession of four, Gentile, world powers that would reign on the earth. There were four kingdoms shown in the dream: Babylon, Medo-Persia, Greece, and finally Rome. Although these empires increased in military prowess, they decreased in splendor. Rome seemed to have the most prominent role of these kingdoms.

In the great image that the king saw in his dream (Dan. 2), Rome was represented by two symbols. One was the iron legs, the other was the feet and toes of iron mixed with clay. The legs of iron represent ancient Rome, and the feet and toes represent the future Roman empire consisting of a ten-nation confederacy. This future coalition of nations will consist of countries of the geographic sphere of ancient Rome.

Although there is some debate over exactly who these ten nations will be, we are certain that ten nations shall rise which will be the foundation for the kingdom of the beast. Even though military strength will be an attribute of the beast's kingdom (symbolized by the iron), it will also be weak, as well as divided. This fact is recorded in Daniel 2:41–43.

> And whereas thou sawest the feet and toes, part of potters clay, and part of iron, the kingdom shall be divided; but there shall be in it of the strength of the iron, forasmuch as thou sawest the iron mixed with miry clay. And as the toes of the feet were part of iron, and part of clay, so the kingdom shall be partly strong, and partly broken. And whereas thou sawest iron mixed with miry clay, they shall mingle themselves with the seed of men: but they shall not cleave one to another, even as iron is not mixed with clay.

From this passage we can conclude that this kingdom will be strong, yet weak; one, but divided; and together, yet not cohesive. We can also see that both the iron and the clay aspects of the kingdom will have very strong interactions with the world populace.

One interpretation of the iron and clay symbology is that the Roman Imperium (the iron) mixed with the popular will (the clay) was fickle and easily molded. Historically, certain commentators have said this came to pass under the constitutional monarchies, in which the republic of France and despotism of Turkey covered the sphere of ancient Roman rule. Although this is an interesting interpretation of these symbols, and it's probably historically accurate to a certain degree; I believe that there is a more plausible interpretation of these symbols that the Bible itself backs up concerning the identity of the miry clay.

If one is to get headed in the right direction with the interpretation of these symbols, one must first consider that just as iron is opposite of clay, so must there be opposite elements in the kingdom of the beast. This means that both will have opposing ideologies and unreconcilable differences while squeezed into the same political arena.

According to the Scriptures, both iron and clay will have great influence over the earth, both politically and economically. In the eyes of the world's populace, both will have special interest groups that are partial to the agenda of either "the iron" or "the clay." This is indicated where the passage says, "they shall mingle themselves with the seed of men, but they shall not cleave one to another." The word mingle comes from the Chaldean word *ar-ab*, which means to commingle, or to mix. It corresponds to the Hebrew word *aw-rab*; which means to braid, to intermix, or to traffic. It is clear both aspects of this kingdom will have their share of the earth's populace, but they themselves will not be a cohesive unit.

Since these two will have great authority on the earth, both aspects of this kingdom will compete for control of the masses. This competition will ultimately set the stage for a fatal conflict between the two. Under the iron fist of the kingdom of the beast, the Anti-christ will rule by forced compliance demanding to be worshiped under the threat of death. He will force those on the earth to receive the mark of the beast, without which no one will be able to buy or sell anything (Rev. 13:1-18). Under the rule of this tyrannical dictatorship, the world will be whipped into submission under history's worst dictator.

On the other hand there will be the alluring influence on the earth who will use demonically inspired seduction instead of forced compliance. Intrinsically and deeply rooted in the hearts of fallen man is the desire to fulfill the lusts of the flesh. Thrill seeking, the pursuit of pleasure, and the desire for uninhibited indulgence reigns in the hearts of unregenerate people. New and improved ways to express their state of depravity become the priorities of life.

This state of moral degeneration that mankind would find itself in during the last days was addressed by the Apostle Paul in 2 Timothy 3:1-4.

> Know also, that in the last days perilous times shall come. For men shall be lovers of their own selves, covetous, boasters, proud, blasphemers, disobedient to parents, unthankful, unholy, Without natural affection, trucebreakers, false accusers, incontinent, fierce, despisers of those that are good, Traitors, heady, highminded, lovers of pleasure more than the lovers of God.

Although the beast will have an iron foot on the necks of the people, ridgid dictatorship will be no match for the sweet fragrance of spellbinding seduction of the great whore, Babylon the great.

In Revelation 17, John tells us about the great whore. One of the angels having the vials of the wrath of God engaged John in a conversation. The angel began to show John the judgment of the great whore, Babylon. It was said of the great whore that she sits upon many waters in whom the kings of the earth have committed fornication and the inhabitants of the earth were made drunk with the wine of her fornication. John was then carried into the wilderness where he saw a woman carried by a scarlet colored beast having seven heads and ten horns.

> And the woman was arrayed in purple and scarlet colour, and decked with gold and precious stones and pearls, having a golden cup in her hand full of abominations and filthiness of her fornication: And upon her forehead was a name written, MYSTERY BABYLON THE GREAT, THE MOTHER OF HARLOTS, AND ABOMINATIONS OF THE EARTH. (Rev. 17:4-5)

Let's examine this passage closely. First, let's look at verse 3, where we see the woman sitting on the back of the scarlet-colored beast, which has seven heads and ten horns. As I discussed earlier, the symbol of the scarlet-colored beast is a historical, geo-political, as well as futuristic symbol for Satan's worldwide kingdom. The ten horns will be the last form of Satanic empire, of this age, which will be headed up by the Anti-christ.

As we look at this beast, we see that the woman (Babylon the great) is riding on the back of the beast. This certainly tells us that there will be a union of the two; in fact while the woman rides the beast, they're both headed in the same direction, or at least to some extent share a common objective. This symbol also shows us that the kingdom of the beast shall be burdened with the great whore.

In comparison with the beast, the great whore, Babylon, will be just the opposite of the kingdom of the beast. The beast is hideous in appearance, a wild and voracious animal. Whereas the whore will be glamorously appareled, decked in expensive jewelry. The beast is masculine, strong, and ferocious. The whore is feminine and seductive. The beast will root up three kings by their roots, and his kingdom will be given to him. The great whore commits fornication with the kings of the earth, controlling them by spiritual and political promiscuity. The beast will have great military prowess. The whore seduces through great wealth and riches. The beast reigns by cruel dictatorship. The whore will control the international commerce and influence. Just as Daniel predicted, the beast will be the iron; the great whore, Babylon, will be the clay. At first they will have somewhat of a union, but as iron and clay will not cleave one to the other, neither will these diametrically opposed political forces.

In the natural realm, women have never been as strong physically as men have. Therefore they have always used seduction to weaken even the strongest of men. Through seduction women have destroyed and conquered great kingdoms and have been the controlling force behind many kingdoms. Because the great whore is seen riding on the beast, it could very well be interpreted that she will at least feel she is in some control of both political entities. This can be seen in Revelation 18:7. "How much she

hath glorified herself, and lived deliciously, so much torment and sorrow give her: for she saith in her heart, I sit
queen, and am no widow, and shall see no sorrow."

But, the great whore Babylon shall meet her fate suddenly by a lethal fiery attack. This is seen in Revelation
17:16. "And the ten horns which thou sawest upon the
beast, these shall hate the whore, and shall make her
desolate and naked, and shall eat her flesh, and burn her
with fire."

In Revelation 18:18–19, another view of the destruction of the great whore is seen. "And cried when they saw
the smoke of her burning, saying, What city is like unto
this great city! And they cast dust on their heads, and
cried, weeping and wailing, saying, Alas, alas that great
city, wherein were made rich all that had ships in the sea
by reason of her costliness! for in one hour is she made
desolate."

From this account the ten-nation confederacy doesn't
sound like they will appreciate being burdened with
Babylon riding on their back. According to 2 Thessalonians
2:4, the beast will want supreme worship as God. However, this will be philosophically contested by the seductive powers of the whore, who mesmerizes her victims
with the wine of her fornication. Because of her lavish life
style, all that commit fornication with her will become
captive by her intoxicating wealth and pleasure. Therefore, Babylon will be the earth's only competing influence
with the kingdom of the beast. Although Babylon may
have the illusion of control, the kingdom of the beast will
suddenly turn on her and destroy her in one hour. Just
as it would be very easy for a strong man to overpower
a defenseless woman, so shall the beast suddenly overpower that great city Babylon.

The Great City

As we continue our study of Babylon, one of the
questions that often arises is, "Will Babylon the City be
rebuilt?" According to the prophets of the Old Testa-

ment, and coupled with the information given to us by
the New Testament, I will submit a solid case based on
the Scriptures and not theology. To answer the question
will Babylon be rebuilt, we need to continue our study of
Revelation 17.

In the book of Revelation, Babylon is referred to as
a literal city seven times. According to the Scriptures
Babylon is an actual place of great international commerce, trade, and business. Merchants of the earth shall
be made rich through the abundance of her delicacies,
and shall greatly lament her destruction.

Babylon shall be rich in natural resources, such as
gold, silver, precious stones, expensive fabrics, wood,
industrial metals, and oil. Babylon shall be an entertainment center, and an international resort and get away,
full of all sorts of leisure and every evil pleasure imaginable. Demonically inspired lust shall reign in the streets
of Babylon, as the world's rich and famous flock there to
express their perverted desires and lusts of every sort.
Drugs, sex, and even the souls of men will be bought and
sold there. Occult and demonic activity will be high, as
people will worship the very seducing spirits that are
behind Babylon's corrupt magnetism (Rev. 18:9-24).

Man, what a place—Babylon will be similar to San
Francisco, New York, Las Vegas, Rio de Janeiro,
Copenhagen, Bangkok, Amsterdam and Singapore all in
one! No wonder the beast will be envious of her great
influence over the people. Babylon's great splendor, lavish delicacies, and her intoxicating seduction will have the
kings of the earth drunk with the wine of her fornication.
The world leaders and the rich and powerful will undoubtedly be torn between forced loyalty to the beast,
and the pursuit of pleasure and filthy lucre that Babylon
will offer.

Many have set forth to identify Babylon. Some say it's
actually Rome. Some have said it's the United States.
Some say it's just a religious system. Some say it's the
Roman Catholic Church. Many say Babylon is exactly

174   *Dennis J. Woods*

what the Bible says it's not. No matter what anyone says,
the Bible says that Babylon is a city. Don't you think that
God knows the difference between a country, a religious
system, and a city?

Yes, Babylon will be such a great city that the people
of the earth will love the pleasures she will offer. With her
deceptive beauty she will become the habitation of every
evil and foul spirit imaginable. Right in the midst of her
lavish lewdity the beast shall order a preemptive attack
(possibly nuclear) on Babylon destroying her in one hour.
From her burning ashes, Babylon will never rise up again,
nor will ever be inhabited again by man or beast! Now
that we know the end of Babylon, let's take a look at the
beginning of "Babylon the great."

The Tower of Babel

Thousands of years ago, after the waters of the great
flood had receded, the descendants of Noah began to
repopulate the earth. Noah had three sons whose names
were Shem, Ham and Japheth. Ham had four sons and
one of them was named Cush. Cush had six sons and one
of them was named Nimrod. Nimrod was a mighty man
in the earth, and was also know as "the mighty hunter"
before the Lord. Nimrod founded and built the cities of
Erech, Accad, Calneh, and Babel, which were all in the
plain of Shinar (Gen. 10:8-10). Nimrod's kingdom also
extended into Assyria, in which he is also credited with
founding the city of Nineveh.

After the flood God wanted man to spread out upon
the face of the whole earth. At this time the people were
of all one language. It came to pass that many journeyed
to the east and settled in the plain of Shinar. Under the
rulership of Nimrod, the people came together to build
a city in the plain of Shinar that would have a tower in
it that could reach into heaven.

Nimrod and the people were interested in making a
name for themselves and becoming established there in
Shinar, fearing that they would be scattered abroad. There-

fore in rebellion against God's wishes for man to spread out on the face of the earth, Nimrod ordered the people to make bricks for a tower that could reach into heaven.

The Lord became interested in the tower that Nimrod was building; therefore, he came down to see it. The Lord found that the people were all in one accord, and of one language. So, the Lord said that nothing could be restrained from these people that they have set out to do because they were as one. So, the Lord confused their language, and scattered them abroad upon the face of the earth. Therefore the name of the place was called Babel, because the Lord *confused* their language (Gen. 11:1-9).

Out of the spirit of pride and in the witchcraft of rebellion, Nimrod's attempt to reach God in his own efforts, and establish a name for himself, ended in a state of confusion, which is the definition of Babel. Although Babel was no more, the roots of rebellion were planted deep. And, up from the seeds of pride and rebellion in the plain of Shinar rose the city of Babylon.

Babylon the City

Because of her roots, the city of Babylon has always been thought of as the symbol of confusion brought on by wickedness; however, the name Babylon actually means, the gate of God. Babylon is located in Shinar, where the city of Babel was built. The actual location is currently marked by the ruin mounds of Babel, six miles northeast of the town of Hillah and about fifty miles south of modern-day Baghdad in Iraq. Today, along the mighty Euphrates River, ruins of this ancient city can be seen for several square miles.

Ancient Babylon was a greatly fortified city. It had two citadels, in the north and south of the city. Both of these citadels had forty-foot high, Ishtar gates. Babylon had a great defense system that incorporated two sets of fortified walls. The inner wall was twenty-one feet thick, and reinforced with towers at sixty-foot intervals. The outer wall was eleven feet in width, with protruding towers. Outside the walls was a brick-lined, quay wall to contain the waters of the Euphrates River. This acted as their flood defense.

King Nebuchadnezzar augmented Babylon's defenses by adding another outer wall, which enclosed his summer palace. This wall was in the northern end of the city and ran for seventeen miles to defend the plain and the outskirts of the city. Later writers say the outer walls ran for forty-two miles, with a middle wall having the height of three hundred feet, with towers extending upwards of 420 feet. Still other historians say that the walls formed a circuit of fifty-six miles.

Babylon was a city given to much idolatry. In both citadels, the Ishtar gates were used for the sacred procession way where many of their pagan rituals were held. There were many temples to its many pagan deities such as Marduk the city's prime deity, and many open air shrines to Babylon's other chief deity, Ishtar (more on her later).

The Fall of Babylon

King Nebuchadnezzar added considerably to Babylon's defenses because he foresaw that his greatest threat would come from the Medes on his eastern front. After his death in 562 B.C., there followed a steadily weakening regime. Great inflation brought on by increased military spending and an extensive public works program, started by King Nebuchadnezzar, amounted to widespread famine. There were also coup attempts and other forms of political unrest that began to plague this city.

In 539 B.C., the Persian army led by Ugbaru, the district governor of Gutium, defeated the Babylonian army at Sippar. This general entered into Babylon without a fight. The ease of the Babylonian conquest was the result of the Persian's diversion of the Euphrates River which rendered Babylonian flood defenses useless. Without active flood defenses, the Persian army was able to enter the city via the dried up river bed. Belshazzar, the son of

Nebuchadnezzar, and the co-regent of Babylon were slain during this non-contested invasion.

On 29 October 539 B.C., Cyrus entered Babylon amid public rejoicing. After Cyrus declared himself king of Babylon, he set his son, Cambyess as viceroy in Babylon, until his death in 522 B.C. Then Darius the Mede ruled in Babylon, (Dan. 5:31) but his rule was often contested by Babylonians (Chaldeans) who controlled various parts of the city. Therefore Darius introduced some very rigid royal control with local administrative reforms to aid in curbing corruption, and established a system of couriers between Babylon and other capitols.

During the reign of Xerxes (485-465 B.C.), in his fourth year as king of Babylon, there was another uprising staged by the Chaldeans. Although this uprising was suppressed, it was done with cruelty and caused great damage to the city. The successor of Xerxes had little time or money to repair much of the damage done to Babylon. Amid their lengthy and expansive wars with the Greeks, irrigation work was neglected. Also, a diversion of trade on the main Persian road from Sardis to Susa further added to the decline of influence of Babylon.

In October 331 B.C., Alexander the Great was welcomed by the Babylonians (Chaldeans) after their defeat of the Medes. Alexander then proclaimed himself king of Babylon and planned extensive renovations of Babylon, but after he returned from the east he suddenly died on 13 June 323 B.C. After Alexander's death the struggles of his generals further left Babylon in great want. With the building of a new capitol city in Seleucia on the Tigris River, Babylon slipped further into decline.

This brief history of the ancient city of Babylon is certainly necessary, when considering the future city of Babylon found in the book of Revelation. As we covered the rise and fall of Babylon, we can certainly see why it was referred to as the head of gold in Daniel 2 and the lion in Daniel 7. There is more to consider concerning Babylon beyond what the historians tell us because there are several prophecies concerning Babylon found in the Old Testament which tell us of her future destruction. If one is going to have clear understanding on Babylon, particularly the Babylon recorded in Revelation, one must refer to the prophets Isaiah and Jeremiah.

From Isaiah's perspective, the defeat of the Babylonians by the Medes and the Persians, was certainly prophesied (Isa. 13:17-22, 21:1-10). This was fulfilled when Belshazzar saw the handwriting on the wall, and was slain that night by the invading Medes, after they diverted the Euphrates River and walked into Babylon uncontested (Dan. 5:28-31).

Although as prophesied Babylon did fall from the excellency of the Chaldeans to the Medes and the Persians, parts of that prophecy were not fulfilled in that campaign. When the Medes and the Persians took over Babylon they did not destroy it; they ruled it for many years. The Medes and Persians ruled over Babylon from at least 539 B.C. to 331 B.C. Yes, the Medes and Persians did take Babylon suddenly as prophesied, but Isaiah describes the exact way Babylon was to be destroyed.

According to Isaiah 13:19-20, we have the prophetic account of the destruction of Babylon. "And Babylon, the glory of the kingdoms, the beauty of the Chaldees' excellency, shall be as when God overthrew Sodom and Gomorrah. It shall never be inhabited, neither shall it be dwelt in from generation to generation . . ."

The prophet Jeremiah also echoes this same prophetic scene in his prophecy of Babylon's destruction. "As God overthrew Sodom and Gomorrah and the neighbour cities thereof, saith the Lord; so shall no man abide there, neither shall any son of man dwell therein" (Jer. 50:40).

According to Genesis 19:24, Sodom and Gomorrah were rained on by fire and brimstone from heaven. Their destruction was by fire, and was totally devastating. When Babylon was overtaken by the Medes and Persians, there wasn't even a fight. The Medes and the Persians did not burn Babylon out of existence. For example, Jeremiah

50:13 tells us because of the "wrath of the Lord," it shall not be inhabited, but it shall be wholly desolate.

In God's careful choice of words, He was letting us know that there was yet a future destruction of Babylon, and that the Mede and Persian invasion only partially fulfilled this prophecy. The passage clearly tells us that the "wrath of God" shall be the reason that Babylon will not be inhabited again. This couldn't possibly have been fulfilled with the Mede and Persian invasion because they themselves occupied Babylon for almost two hundred years afterwards.

In Jeremiah 51:25-26, 29, we get another glimpse of future judgment of Babylon.

> And I will stretch out my hand upon thee, and roll thee down from the rocks, and will make thee a burnt mountain. And they shall not take of thee a stone for a corner, nor a stone for foundations; but thou shalt be desolate for ever, saith the Lord. And the land shall tremble and sorrow: for every purpose of the Lord shall be performed against Babylon, to make the land of Babylon a desolation without an inhabitant.

Still another account of the future destruction of Babylon is further recorded by Jeremiah.

> Then shalt thou say, O Lord, thou hast spoken against this place, to cut it off, that none shall remain in it, neither man nor beast, but that it shall be desolate for ever, And it shall be, when thou hast made an end of reading this book, that thou shalt bind a stone to it, and cast it into the midst of Euphrates: And thou shalt say, Thus shall Babylon sink, and shall not rise from the evil that I will bring upon her. (Jer. 51:62-64)

There is absolutely no way that this prophecy was fulfilled by the Mede and Persian invasion. After the Mede and Persian empire ruled in Babylon then the Greeks took it over (Dan. 8:3-9, 15-22). After the death of

Alexander the Great, the Grecian empire was divided into four parts, but Seleucid remained in the Babylonian region and later moved his capital up near the Tigris River. During the Seleucid era when all documents were dated, documents on clay from a priestly school in Babylon are dated as far as A.D. 100. This is why many believe that Peter greets the church that was at Babylon (1 Pet. 5:13). There were also devout Jews who were from Mesopotamia (Babylonia) in Jerusalem on the day of Pentecost (Acts 2:1, 9).

Because many theologians look at just the one level of prophetic fulfillment (Babylonian conquest by the Medes and the Persians) as being the total fulfilling of all the prophecy concerning Babylon, they totally discount any future fulfillment. The Scriptures clearly tell us that there was a church at Babylon in Peter's day. Hundreds of years had already expired after the prophecies concerning Babylon were supposed to have been fulfilled; yet, people were still living there.

It's funny, but because of commentators' opinions concerning Babylon's prophetic fulfillment, they completely discount 1 Peter 5:13, as not actually meaning Babylon, but Rome. They also give no credence to the book of Revelation's account of the future destruction of Babylon. They claim it's just a "religious system" with Rome as it headquarters, although seven times Revelation calls Babylon an actual city. As far as many are concerned, Babylon is just the system of false religion that the beast will rule over from Rome. But, according to Jeremiah 51:29, "Every purpose of the Lord shall be performed against Babylon, to make the *land* of Babylon a desolation without an inhabitant." Again with hundreds of years of occupation that followed the Medeo-Persian invasion, this prophecy has not yet been totally fulfilled.

As Jeremiah spoke of the land of Babylon being judged, so does the prophet Zechariah speak against the land. Almost twenty years after Cyrus walked into Babylon and declared himself as the king, the prophet Zechariah was writing his prophecies, from approximately 520 to 518 B.C. The prophecies of the Medes and Persians against Babylon had already come to pass. However Zechariah gives us a look at a yet future prophecy, concerning the land of Babylon.

In Zechariah 5, the prophet sees an *ephah* which is a container for measuring dry goods. An ephah has the capacity of about four gallons. In Zechariah 5:7-11 the prophet tells us this.

> And, Behold, there was lifted up a talent of lead: and this is a woman that sitteth in the midst of the ephah. And he said, This is wickedness. And he cast it into the midst of the ephah; and he cast the weight of lead upon the mouth thereof. Then lifted I up mine eyes, and looked, and behold there came out two women, and the wind was in their wings, for they had wings like the wings of a stork: and they lifted up the ephah between the earth and the heaven. Then said I to the angel, that talked with me, Whither do these bear the ephah? And he said to me, To build it an house in the land of Shinar: and it shall be established, and set there upon her own base.

Shinar is the plain where Nimrod founded the city of Babel, from where the city of Babylon rose up and took her role in world history. Zechariah couldn't have been referring to the prophecies concerning the Medes and Persians, as it had already been fulfilled by this time.

The Rebuilding of Babylon

During the late 1980s I was living in Chicago, working for the U.S. Justice Department. I got up one morning and was watching the "Today Show" starring Bryant Gumble, who announced a news segment on the rebuilding of the ancient city of Babylon. At the time I was absolutely flabbergasted, because I knew the significance that it had prophetically. Since that time, I've found out that the Iraqi government has had restoration work going on in Babylon for some time now.

Modern-day Iraq is the ancient site of many historical cities—cities such as Nineveh, Babel, Mesopotamia and Babylon. Iraq is one the world's petroleum-producing nations, and is a member of the thirteen-nation cartel. The Iraqi government and people are devout haters of Israel, and are among the Islamic fundamentalists that have declared the Islamic Jihad (holy war) against Israel.

The Iraqi military machine is primarily supplied by what used to be the Soviet Union. All sorts of Soviet arms have been stockpiled in Iraq for years and were in action against the coalition forces in the Desert Storm War. Persia's (Iran and Iraq) military relationship with Gog and Magog is a matter of biblical record in Ezekiel 38 and 39. For the first time the western world became familiar with the term SCUD missile as Saddam Hussein launched scud after scud at Israel.

For a long time now, Baghdad has been the capital of Iraq, but the Iraqi government will probably switch its capital to Babylon. It is said of Saddam Hussein that he believes he is the reincarnation of King Nebuchadnezzar, and has a vision to restore the excellency of Babylon to the level of its former glory.

Although Iraq switching its capital to Babylon may seem to be far-fetched, it's no longer a long shot. The restoration of Babylon may be quite feasible, considering the amounts of damage suffered from American smart bombs and cruise missiles during the Desert Storm War and other air raids since.

However this comes about, Iraq and the city of Babylon have an appointment with destiny and no amount of theological denial will stop what's prophesied from occurring. Yes, the kingdom of the beast will be in the same league with Babylon as this city rides upon the back of the beast. Yet the beast will find himself in competition with the intoxicating pleasures and wealth offered by the great whore, Babylon. Therefore, he shall hate the whore.

Just as Daniel pictured it in his prophecy, the beast will be the iron, Babylon will be the clay. Both will mingle themselves with the seed of men, but they shall not cleave one to the other. Then Babylon will suddenly be destroyed by the beast. In one hour she shall be burned with fire and brought to naught never to rise again (Rev. 18:9-24).

The World's Oldest Profession—Babylon, Part II

The Mother of Harlots

Many of today's expositors have written much commentary on Babylon as the great whore and mother of harlots. Although, they would probably stick to the traditional interpretations concerning Babylon's prophecies as being fulfilled already, I have just shown you how the prophecies of Isaiah and Jeremiah couldn't possibly be fulfilled in their entirety already. However, there is one point of interest that I, as well as others agree on, and that is Babylon also represents a system of false religions.

The false religion aspect of Babylon has been the point of much controversy over the years. According to some theological minds, Babylon represents apostate Christianity. For many this has usually meant the Roman Catholic Church, sighting her many non-biblical pagan practices. They also cite the Catholic church as Mystery Babylon the Great, because Rome, or Vatican City, is the capital of the church. The Roman Catholic Church has worldwide authority and great wealth and power, even having its own ambassadors and international banks as if it were its own country, and in a sense it is.

However, it is not the focus of this chapter to try to identify the Catholics with Babylon the great. But, I am going to do a study of the religions that began in ancient Babylon which still have great influence even in today's Christianity. Believe it or not, many of Christianity's customs and traditions have Babylon's fingerprints all over them.

In the book of Revelation, Babylon is called the

"Mother of Harlots and Abominations of the Earth." That's because Babylon was the birthplace of many pagan deities. After Satan, "the father of lies" impregnated Babylon with seeds of idolatry and deception, Babylon brought forth (harlot) religious offsprings that whored throughout the whole earth. Babylon was like a sexually transmitted disease that spread rapidly and infected all that fornicated with her.

The most common form of Babylon's religious fornication and occult rituals was expressed in pagan idolatry. Idolatry is defined as the worship of idols or statues, or to worship a person or a thing. Paul warned against idolatry.

> What say I then? that the idol is anything, or that which is offered in sacrifice to idols is anything? But I say, that the things which the Gentiles sacrifice, they sacrifice to devils [demons], and not to God: and I would not that ye should have fellowship with devils. Ye cannot drink the cup of the Lord, and the cup of devils: ye cannot be partakers of the Lord's table and of the table of devils. (1 Cor. 10:19-21)

Paul is clearly telling us that idolatry is really demon worship! Worship of pagan deities was not to be incorporated into Christian worship.

Babylon was also referred to as the "mother of abominations of the earth." The word abomination means something that is detestable, particularly an idol. This definition comes from the Hebrew word *shik-koots*. Another Hebrew word translated abomination in English is *to-ay-baw* which is the feminine active participle of the Hebrew word *taw-ab* which means to loathe or to morally detest and to abhor. The word *to-ay-baw* is the word that was used to describe abhorrent customs and religious practices. This is the word that is used to describe the religious abominations that God showed to Ezekiel.

God showed Ezekiel some abominations that the children of Israel were practicing in God's Temple.

> He said also unto me, Turn thee yet again, and thou shalt see greater abominations that they do. Then he brought me to the door of the gate of the Lord's house which was toward the north; and behold, there sat women weeping for Tammuz. And he brought me into the inner court of the Lord's house, and, behold, at the door of the temple of the Lord, between the porch and the altar, were about five and twenty men, with their backs toward the temple of the Lord, and their faces toward the east; and they worshiped the sun towards the east. (Ezek. 8:13-14, 16)

Here we have an example of customary abominations that had infiltrated God's own temple. In verse 16 we have a picture of the ancient sun worship. They were worshiping the sun in the east (dawn). This is a picture of the ancient sunrise services.

What I would like to call your attention to is verse 14, where it says that the women were weeping for Tammuz. Tammuz was the Sumerian/Babylonian god of summer and vegetation. According to Babylonian custom, Tammuz died and went into the underworld, which is represented by the annual wilting of the crops under the scorching summer sun. Therefore there were annual mourning rites that normally took place in June or July. This is why in Ezekiel 8 the women are seen weeping for Tammuz.

Tammuz's return to the earth brought about another Babylonian god by the name of Ishtar. Ishtar was the goddess of love and fertility. In 1968 the Iraqi Government began reconstruction of the Ishtar Gate, that was in Babylon's southern citadel. There were many open-air shrines in dedication to Ishtar as worship of this pagan deity was widespread. Ishtar was also associated with Venus, and had an alternate role as the morning star.

The worship of Ishtar did not stay within the boarders of Babylon. She was also identified with Isis, the Egyptian goddess of fertility. Isis' symbol was the woman head with two cow's horns that rose above her head and a solar disk in between the two horns. The solar disk represented her association with sun worship, which was prevalent in both Babylonian and Egyptian cultures. Since both Isis and Ishtar were love and fertility goddesses, their worship promoted sexual promiscuity and the expression of lustful love. The cults that followed these deities held celebration ceremonies for Ishtar and Isis during the springtime which represented the time of fertility.

According to some historical recordings, the worship of Isis and her cult penetrated deeply into the Greco-Roman Empires. This cult spread rapidly throughout all of Europe and competed with early Christianity. European cultures were by far pagan, and as Christianity spread through Europe it picked up many pagan rituals, much of which was a compromise to convert pagans to Christianity.

If one were to ask the average Christian, what are the most important Christian holidays? I'm sure they would say, Christmas and Easter. If you would then ask them, "Where did these holidays originate?" They probably wouldn't be able to tell you that. The important thing to realize about both Christmas and Easter is that Jesus Himself didn't institute either one of these holidays. The only observance that Jesus instituted was the "Last Supper." The Lord commanded "This do in remembrance of Me" (Luke 22:19). If Christ did not institute this observances, then who did?

Before I answer that question, let's recap. Ishtar was the Babylonian goddess of love and fertility; she was also associated with Venus and was called the morning star. Ishtar was also worshipped by the Egyptians, under the name of Isis, who was also the goddess of fertility. Isis' image was the woman head with two cow horns, having a solar panel between the horns. Both Ishtar and Isis were related to sun worship, and festivals given by their cults were spring festivals that represented fertility. Ishtar was the wife and sister of Tammuz. According to Babylonian tradition, after the death of Tammuz, Ishtar went into the underworld and raised Tammuz from the dead.

Tammuz also had an Egyptian counterpart named Osiris who was married to Isis. They had a son by the name of Horus, the Egyptian sun god. According to Egyptian mythology, Osiris and Ra were the chief deities of Egyptians. The worship of Osiris (Tammuz) came close to being the universal cult religion just before the advent of Christianity.

Osiris and Ra would offer their cult believers an alternative to the afterlife. The dead could sail over the heavens by day with him by his sacred boat. Then they went through the netherworld by night and would rise daily with him at dawn on the eastern horizon. During the time of the new Egyptian kingdom there was a supporting theology of Osiris and Ra, as the rising sun by day and the night sun which preceded the rebirth. These were the cults that spread throughout Europe and even Asia Minor. For example, Diana of the Ephesians was also a fertility goddess, who was associated with trolls. The little troll cartoons and dolls are all associated with ancient pagan deities that were birthed by the mother of harlots, Babylon.

As I said earlier, Easter was not a holiday instituted by Jesus. Although the word is found in Acts 12:4, the actual Greek word used in the original text is *pas-khah*, which is of Chaldean origin, and is actually translated Passover. The Passover was celebrated in the spring months, either March or April.

Easter probably goes back as far A.D. 154, when the paschal controversy arose concerning the correct date for Easter observances. In any case Easter observances coincided with the observance of the Passover, during the spring equinox. The date is usually the first Sunday after the first full moon which normally comes after March 21st.

Easter has ancient Teutonic (German) roots, as the

"spring goddess" to whom sacrifices were offered up in April. Easter was also the goddess of dawn. Not only does Easter have ancient German roots, but she also has ancient Anglo-Saxon roots as well. In Anglo-Saxon customs, Easter was the goddess of spring, with a month dedicated to her called "Eostur-monath." Whether it be ancient German or Anglo-Saxon, the rendering of Easter is consistent as either the goddess of spring, which is a fertility deity, or the goddess of dawn, which has its roots in sun worship. The pagan fertility aspects of Easter are clearly seen in the Easter eggs and bunny rabbits. Eggs represent new birth, and bunny rabbits represent fertility and rapid reproductivity. Spring was the most appropriate time for these fertility goddesses because the spring was the season for the beginning of new life for both plants and animals.

Just as Osiris and Isis were worshiped at dawn, so was Easter. Just as Isis and Ishtar were fertility goddess, so was Easter. Remember, Osiris was the Egyptian version of Tammuz. It was Tammuz who was raised from the dead by his wife Ishtar. Now you can see why when God saw the wickedness of his people in Ezekiel, chapter 8, He called them great abominations. They were doing these abominations right in God's temple. They were weeping for Tammuz, and worshipping the sun at dawn. Although I don't think you will find many Christians who actually worship these pagan symbols, I do think that it is important to know where these things come from.

Babylon, the mother of harlots and abominations of the earth, birthed many pagan cult religions. Many people of the earth have fornicated with these pagan cult deities, that have even surfaced in Christianity and are still practiced to this day. This is the main reason why many churches are now moving away from calling the day of Christ's Resurrection "Easter" and are rightly referring to it as "Resurrection Day."

Although I may have presented some disturbing information concerning Babylon's harlotry, I chose to use a holiday that's part of Christianity to illustrate how far Babylon's influence has reached. Because the focus of this book is doctrinal and not investigative, I've only done a short study of Babylon. There's much more to tell about Babylon, and the Papal Church's connection to it.

Please remember what the Bible says in Romans, chapter 14; Christians either honor certain days unto the Lord or not honor them unto the Lord. It's according to one's faith. So I'm not saying that you're not saved if you buy your kids an Easter basket on Easter, nor am I saying that Christmas trees will send you to hell. I'm just reiterating the fact that there's nothing new under the sun.

Fifteen
☙☙ ❧❧

Shall He Find Faith

After all has been said and done, after each side has presented their cases, the question still remains, What difference does it make? This question puts me in mind of the film classic *Gone with the Wind*. In the film after the news began to spread that there would be a civil war, many of the South's men were anxious to run off to war against the northern Yankees. Clark Gable's character Rhett Butler brought out the point that the South was not prepared to fight the North. He said that the South did not have an industrialized war machine with cannon factories. One of the young men in the crowd shouted, "Who cares if they have cannons and we don't. What difference does it make?" Rhett Butler replied, "I'm afraid it will make a big difference, to a great many men."

No matter what theory you believe—the bottom line is there will be a "last generation" of Church saints. Whether it's us, our children, or our grandchildren, someone will be "alive and remaining" unto the coming of the Lord. To that generation the times in which they live will be their reality; it will be their here and now. Situations won't be exegetical or technical theories; they will be experiential and very much real.

What difference does it make? That will be an important question to them. They will need to know the truth; they will need to know exactly what their options are. Is a, "Don't worry about it, we won't have to deal with what's coming" attitude a wise one? Will that type of answer prepare them for what could happen if the pre-trib rapture theory is wrong? The fact is, many are being asked to put all their eggs in a basket woven in theories. Many Jews didn't believe their temple would be destroyed and they would go into captivity, either. Many probably said, "God won't let that happen to us," right up until the Babylonians came.

Over the centuries men have consistently failed to realize one thing about God: His thoughts are not our thoughts, and His ways are not our ways. So with this in mind, "What difference does it make?" is a very relevant question, particularly for those who will be living at the time of the rapture. For as it says in Luke, chapter 18, "I tell you that he will avenge them speedily. Nevertheless when the Son of man cometh, shall he find faith on the earth?" (Luke 18:8).

Shall He find faith on the earth? My friends, that is the question. For without faith it is impossible to please God. Faith always takes the position that no matter what shall happen, no matter what men shall do to me, no matter of things present or things to come, it shall be, for God I will live or for God I will die. If a man is not willing to die for his faith (not saying that you will have to), he will compromise if his life is threatened. With many, you won't even have to threaten their lives, just threaten their livelihoods and see how far their religion will take them. Remember what Jesus told the church at Smyrna while they were going through persecution? "Be thou faithful unto death, and I will give thee a crown of Life" (Rev. 2:10). Jesus didn't tell them, "I won't let you suffer." Nor did He tell them, "I won't let you die." Their comfort was not Jesus' focus at all. The Lord's focus was the eternal weight of glory (the crown of life) that they would receive for their faithfulness in the face of severe persecution and death.

You see, when it's your head on the chopping block, when it's your blood that's being spilled, when it's your faith that's being tried, you will soon know where you stand with the Lord. When you are suffering tribulation, whether it's tribulation in the technical or eschatological sense won't be the issue at all. Christians of the 1990s, examine yourselves whether ye be of the faith, lest ye be reprobates. Jesus hasn't come yet, but are you willing to die for the faith? Would you compromise if faced with death? Would you have the same attitude and faith that the Old Testament saints had who died without the promises that we have today?

As we read about the heroic saints found in faith's "Hall of Fame," I would like to call your attention to Hebrews 11:35, "Women received their dead raised to life again: and others were tortured, not accepting deliverance; that they might obtain a better resurrection."

Can you imagine a faith so great, that you would refuse to be freed, but would rather die because of your absolute commitment to Jesus Christ? Can you imagine not fearing anything; whether it be men, demons or the Anti-christ himself? Are we strong saints of God not fearing those that have power to kill just the body, but being committed unto Him that has the power of eternal life? We should be like the three Hebrew boys who told Nebuchadnezzar, "Our God is able to deliver us from the fire, but even if he doesn't we still shall not bow down to the image" (Dan. 3:16-18). These great men of faith realized one thing; God can. But, what if He doesn't? At that point, my friends, it's your faith and the fire.

You see, true faith takes you beyond the cares of this life and transports you into the eternal, unto the things that are not seen. As Paul so eloquently said in 2 Corinthians 4:17–18. "For our light affliction, which is but for a moment, worketh for us a far more exceeding and eternal weight of glory; While we look not at the things which are seen, but at the things which are not seen: for the things which are seen are temporal; but the things which are not seen are eternal."

As I stated earlier, pre-trib theory rests on some bad interpretations of key Scriptures. Although they do have some well-structured arguments, much of it still rests on exegesis instead of substantive biblical ground. In other words, the pre-trib position is highly theoretical. Although they don't come out and say it, pre-trib theory caters to the, "I don't want to suffer" comfortable Christian. This type of professing Christian just wants to float right on through their Christian walk, the fewer trials and tribulations, the better. As I stated earlier, Chuck Swindoll said, "I'm pre-trib, but what if Jesus isn't?" I admire him because he has enough sense to understand that theology does not have the final say so. God does! We must all be able to look at our theories and say, "What if it's not like we think it is?" What if we really do need to think things through again. Are we willing to do so? Unfortunately that's the problem with many of us; we won't budge when it comes to our traditions.

Remember Peter's vision of the sheet and the unclean animals? Even though it was the Lord Himself telling Peter to kill and eat, Peter told the Lord, "Not so." Can you imagine telling the Lord, "Not so"? Tradition will do it to you every time. I remember seeing a Dr. Taylor on a television program called "Today in Bible Prophecy" saying: "Get saved now and be caught up in the rapture or you'll have to go through the tribulation. You can still be saved then, but you might have to die." I must admit that statement made me sick, especially when you consider that the Church was founded in martyrdom and persecution. Although Dr. Taylor's statement may have appeased the ears of many, he couldn't deny the fact that there are tribulation saints in the first resurrection.

Where does such a carnal attitude come from? If we take a look at Peter's response to Jesus after the Lord disclosed that He was going to build His Church, we can see a very subtle force at work. Jesus had told His disciples that He was going to go to Jerusalem and suffer many things from the religious leaders, and be killed (Matt. 16:21-22). Now from the point of human concern, not wanting to see terrible things happen to the Lord, Peter rebuked Him and said, "Be it far from thee!" Peter couldn't see the spiritual significance of Christ's sacrifice. As the Apostle Paul later taught, The things which are seen are temporal. For our light affliction is but for a moment, but worketh for us a far more exceeding weight of eternal glory (2 Cor. 4:17-18). Peter couldn't see the purpose of the sufferings of Christ, and their eternal significance. Peter's response to Jesus' prophesied demise was not unusual. After all, who wants to suffer and die? Therefore, Peter said, "Be it far from thee, Lord" (Matt. 16:22).

During this discourse, it's interesting to note that Jesus didn't rebuke Peter for making his comment. However, the Lord did rebuke Satan, who was manipulating Peter's emotions. That is really ironic because Peter had just had a revelation of Jesus being the Son of God. So Jesus told Satan that he was an offense to Him: for he "savourest" not the things that are of God, but of men. Then Jesus told his disciples the stark reality of the Christian walk.

> If any man, [that includes modern day Christians] will come after me, let him deny himself, and take up *his cross*, and follow me. For whosoever will *save* his life shall lose it: and whosoever will lose his life for my sake shall find it. For what is a man profited, if he shall gain the whole world, and lose his own soul? or what shall a man give in exchange for

his soul? For the Son of man shall come in the
glory of his Father with his angels; and then he
shall reward every man according to his works.
(Matt. 16:24-27) (emphasis mine)

Now you can spiritualize this, you can exegeticalize
this, you can manipulate it, or whatever you want to do,
but you can't change it. Go ahead and say, "This just
pertains to Israel," if you want to. I certainly wouldn't
stake anyone's life on that. The facts remain the same; if
you seek to save your life you will lose it. If you savor the
things of men more that the things of God, you will
compromise. The bottom line is compromise is deadly.
So is teaching people they won't have to suffer.

Now I'm not talking about some harsh treatment of
the body, or some false humility, as Paul speaks of in
Colossians. I'm talking about genuine love for Jesus at
any and all cost. This is why Paul states in Philippians
3:10–11, "That I might know him, and the power of his
resurrection, and the fellowship of his sufferings, being
made conformable to his death; If by any means I might
attain unto the resurrection of the dead."

The Apostle Peter professed the same revelation in 1 Peter
4:12–13. "Beloved, think it not strange concerning the fiery
trial which is to try you, as though some strange thing
happened unto you; But rejoice inasmuch as ye are partakers of Christ's sufferings; that, when his glory shall be
revealed, ye may be glad also with exceeding joy."

When Peter wrote these encouraging words, Christians were being thrown to the lions for entertainment.
Under Nero, Roman coliseums flowed with Christian
blood. The Christians then aren't any deader than the
saints that will be killed by the beast. As a matter of fact
it will be the same kingdom "Rome," just a reconstructed
version. What makes you think this won't happen again?
Are we more the Body of Christ than they were? Are we
holier than they were? Is God a respecter of persons, that
he wouldn't dare let us 1990 Christians go through what

earlier generations of Christians readily accepted and have
already gone through? Christianity began under that
Gentile kingdom, and it will close out under that kingdom.

When God sees our sufferings, He's looking at the
eternal weight of glory, but many of us are thinking about
our own skins. It's literally an opportunity to die for
Jesus. Remember in the book of Acts, how Jesus stood up
to receive Stephen when he was stoned? The Lord was
pleased at this man's faith unto the death. As the Scriptures tell us "Precious in the sight of the Lord is the death
of his saints" (Ps. 116:15).

We're not appointed to the wrath of God, which happens during the day of the Lord, after the abomination
of desolation is in place. This is the pre-wrath rapture
fact.

Let's Analyze the Options

Paul addresses some key issues in 2 Thessalonians
2:3. "For that day [the day of the Lord] shall not come,
except there come a falling away first and the man of sin
be revealed, the son of perdition." As I covered earlier
the word *falling* comes from the Greek word, *ap-os-tas-ee-
ah*, where we get our English word apostasy from. Apostasy means to forsake or to defect from the truth. Although the state of apostasy is detailed in Romans, chapter 1; 1 Timothy, chapter 4; 2 Timothy, chapter 3, and
other Scriptures, moral depravation is not the only cau-
sation of apostasy.

As pre-trib doctrine teaches, the Church will not go
through any part of the seventieth week of Daniel. But,
what if that's wrong? Suppose millions of unsuspecting
Christians are still here. What are the options under this
scenario? The following scenario I'm bringing up warrants looking into.

The Modern-day Thessalonians

What if one day we all wake up, and there he is, the
man of sin, inaugurating the seven-year covenant of peace.

Israel goes back to animal sacrifices and daily oblations in their rebuilt temple. Because of the perimeters set by pre-trib theory, those of that doctrinal persuasion would be faced with some faith-crushing realities.

They would believe that they have entered into the day of the Lord. That's because their theory teaches that the whole seventieth week is the day of the Lord, the time of God's wrath. This is the same thing that happened to the congregation at Thessalonica. Someone had written a false letter claiming to be from Paul saying that the day of the Lord was already upon them. This caused serious problems for them. They were "shaken in mind and troubled," (confused and gripped in fear). Paul had already taught them that they wouldn't go through the wrath of God, but now they found themselves in the midst of what they believed to be the day of the Lord. Just as the Thessalonians, modern Christians would first have to deal with the uncertainty caused by being taught the wrong thing. This would immediately begin to eat away at other areas of their faith.

If they thought they were in the day of the Lord, then, certainly to some, it would mean that they must have missed the rapture. Why? Because the Bible clearly teaches that the rapture will happen prior to the day of the Lord. Finding themselves in the midst of the seventieth week, what hope would they have if they believe they've missed their blessed hope? As the Bible records, this was another doctrine that was destroying people's faith. Paul had to write in 2 Timothy about the doctrine of Philetus and Hymenæus, that taught that the resurrection had occurred already, which overthrew the faith of the people (2 Tim. 2:18). Paul had to also address a similar doctrine in 1 Corinthians 15:12, which said there was no resurrection. Paul clearly tells us that without the hope of the resurrection, preaching, our faith, and this life is all in vain. The thought of missing the resurrection would be devastating to any generation of Christians, just as it was in Paul's day.

Being in the midst of the day of the Lord and now realizing that they had been taught the wrong thing or had missed the rapture would result in overwhelming fear in the face of severe persecution. With the real possibility of death, modern Christians would be faced with the historic reality that many generations of Christians lived with. Many Christians will defect left and right, just as the Bible says; there will be a falling away first. Why? Because the seventieth week will have started and the Church will still be here. How many of those unsuspecting Christians who thought they would be raptured away would stand if their lives were threatened? How many would face starvation, or live in the streets? How many could stand to see their families go in want. These are realities that past Christians in the Body of Christ lived with. Go to your library and get one of the books of martyrs. Read about the earlier Church saints that endured to the end. It's just in our modern western, comfort zone, where there's a church on every corner, that we haven't seen these types of circumstances. There are countries on the earth today where you could lose your life, property, or be thrown in prison because of the name of Jesus.

Think about it. This scenario that I've just put forth is not far-fetched at all. Why? It warrants looking into because the pre-trib position is a theory. Moreover, saints have already experienced the above situations as evidenced by the Scriptures in Corinthians, Thessalonians, and Timothy. It's not far-fetched at all. Remember there's nothing new under the sun.

Things are Changing

Remember what Jesus said in the parable of the sower and the seed, concerning those who would fall away? "Some fell upon stony places, where they had not much earth: and forthwith they sprung up, because they had no deepness of earth: And when the sun was up, they were scorched; and because they had no root, they withered away. And some fell among thorns; and the thorns sprung up, and choked them" (Matt. 13:5-7).

Jesus then interprets these parables, beginning in verse 20 the passage says:

> But he that received the seed into stony places, the same is he that heareth the word, and anon with joy receiveth it; Yet hath he not root in himself, but dureth for a while: for when tribulation or persecution ariseth because of the word, by and by he is offended. He also that received seed among the thorns is he that hearth the word: and the care of this world, and the deceitfulness of riches, choke the word, and he becometh unfruitful. (Matt. 13:20-22)

Some theologians will tell you that the tribulation and persecution in these passages is not in an eschatological sense. But, to that I would say; "I wouldn't stake my life on their theories." Theologians didn't die for me; Jesus did, and I will believe the Bible before I believe their exegetical postulations. Is "believing the Word of God" in the above passage non-eschatological sense also? The saints in Revelation 20:4-6 certainly didn't think so, because that's why they were beheaded, for keeping the Word of God and the testimony of Jesus Christ. They obviously didn't fall into the category of those that had no root. Neither did they wither away in the face of persecution. Remember, the Apostle John was also persecuted for the "Word of God" just as the Revelation, chapter 20 saints were. If faithfulness to the Word is eschatological, how come persecution and tribulation in Matthew 13 can't be? The principle that Jesus laid down in Matthew 13 concerning faithfulness to the Word doesn't change in any age, which includes the tribulation. The truth never changes because the Word of God never changes, no matter what our doctrines teach.

In Philippians 2:15–16 Paul encourages the saints to hold forth the Word of God "in the midst of a crooked and perverse nation, among whom ye shine as lights in the world; Holding forth the word of life that I may rejoice in the day of Christ . . ."

Just as the Lord said, we are the light of the world, and we are in the midst of a crooked and sinful nation. As the world gets exceedingly sinful and as the professing Church compromises more and more with the world, true saints will be the God consciousness or the light that will illuminate the sinful state of their societies. Christian ethics will be the only thing that gets in the way of evil people expressing their immorality. Because we are the salt of the earth, our presence will burn and irritate society's sores of sin, just like pouring salt into an open wound.

Therefore, Christians will become the target of increasingly intensified persecution. Just look around us here in America. The true Church will be the only ones who will tell the world that they must repent and turn away from sin. That message will not go over well in a world bent on doing evil. Being ostracized, ridiculed, harassed, and mocked will be too much for the Christian with no deepness of root to handle. I believe that all that I have mentioned in this chapter will also figure into the falling away from the faith, spoken of in 2 Thessalonians.

As more and more televangelists tell the Church that this will be the year of the rapture, they are simply adding to the anxiety. Right now there is a book out that says the rapture will be in 1994. Others says 1996, 1997, 1998, and certainly by the year 2000. Millions of Christians having their heads filled with all these dates and years are setting people up with the "We won't be here" mentality. They have become so prophetically vertical, that they aren't being horizontally realistic. Certainly the prophesied "scoffers and mockers" will seize an opportunity to criticize the date-and-year-setting Christians, and the Church as a whole. This may be one of the reasons why the mockers shall come saying, "Where is the promise of his coming?"

What the Church must be ever mindful of is that judgment must first begin at the house of the Lord (1 Pet.

4:17). Do you think the Lord is pleased with our denomi-
national separation, our fad doctrines and traditions, the
lasciviousness, the pride, the racism, the divorce, and the
scandal? Have we all come to the unity of the faith? Are
we above being seriously persecuted? There are ordained
ministers that don't even believe that the Bible is the
inerrant Word of God.

The tables are turning, my brothers and sisters. In
America one can't mention God in the schools or in
government arenas, but one can in Russia. It's no longer
freedom of religion in this country, but freedom *from*
religion is the order of the day. I'm afraid persecution
will be the only way we will drop all of our carnality.
When Israel was only seventy strong they went into Egypt
and were blessed there and multiplied exceedingly. But,
Egypt was not the place that God had chosen to give to
them for an inheritance. Although Egypt had been the
place of blessing for so many years, it became a place of
bondage, trials, and persecution. Yet, they faithfully waited
for a deliverer some four hundred years. Yes, it was
through persecution that God chose to take them into
the promised land. Just as God says in Isaiah 48:10-11,
"Behold, I have refined thee, but not with silver: I have
chosen thee in the furnace of affliction. For mine own
sake, even for mine own sake, will I do it: for how should
my name be polluted? and I will not give my glory unto
another."

Brothers and sisters, the time will come when it won't
make much difference if you're Baptist or Methodist,
Lutheran or Church of God in Christ, Apostolic or Evangelical. All the world will care about is if you are an open
Christian who won't compromise, you'll be a threat to
them and will suffer persecution.

Right here in America we shall see persecution of the
Church. The Body of Christ began in persecution, and I
believe the Bible tells us the Church will close out in
persecution. Ironically, times of persecution are not only

times of God's purification, but they are also times of great Church growth. Although evil forces will oppose the Church, an innumerable amount of people from all over the world will be saved and come out of great tribulation.

Christ will rapture the Church before the day of the Lord comes; that's a fact. However, it won't be a minute before the fullness of the Gentiles is come in. My dear readers think about it; if I'm wrong, we'll be raptured up anyway before the seventieth week comes, and no one is hurt. But, what if pre-trib theory is wrong? Will you remain faithful to the end?

According to the Scriptures there is only one unforgivable sin and that's blasphemy of the Holy Spirit (Matt. 12:31-32). I believe that Revelation 14:9-12 gives us a form of this unpardonable sin.

> And the third angel followed them, saying with a loud voice, If any man worship the beast and his image, and receive his mark in his forehead or in his hand, The same shall drink of the wine of the wrath of God, which is poured without mixture into the cup of his indignation; and shall be tormented with fire and brimstone in the presence of the holy angels and in the presence of the Lamb: And the smoke of their torment ascendeth up for ever and ever: and they have no rest day nor night, who worship the beast and his image, and whosoever receiveth the mark of his name. Here is the patience of the saints: here are they that keep the commandments of God, and the faith of Jesus.

When the Son of man cometh shall He find faith in the earth? That will be the real question. What difference will it make if pre-trib theory is wrong? It will mean Christians won't be gone during the seventieth week and may very well have to die for their faith under the persecution of the beast. Although millions of believers have died over the centuries, those living during the seventieth week will be different because of one biblical stipulation.

If you fall away in this scenario and receive the mark of
the beast, you will spend eternity in hell. That's what
difference it will make. The Bible says that all those whose
names were not written in the Lamb's book of life shall
worship the beast (Rev. 13:8). This means that those of us
that are truly saved will not worship the beast. The problem is, none of us really knows who's saved and who's
not. The wolves in sheep's clothing are in practically every congregation. During the church age, wheat and tares
grow together. More often than not, we don't know the
difference between the tares and the wheat.

The Bible says that the beast shall make war with the
saints and overcome them (Rev. 13:7; Dan. 7:21-22). You
can call those persecuted by the beast Israel if you want
to, but understand that the Bible doesn't say that; men
do. Whatever generation is here when this happens,
whether it's today, the year 2000, or a hundred years
from now, will be a generation of saints that will have to
deal with those circumstances. What difference will it
make? An eternal one, if they fall away and yield to the
dictates of the beast; they will have an unpardonable sin
and an unchangeable destiny in the lake of fire.

I have not given you a theology that sounds good,
but rather the truth from the Word of God as He revealed it to me, backed by an abundance of Scripture. No
matter how dark it gets, no matter how many die for the
faith, remember the words of the Apostle Paul,

> Who shall separate us from the love of Christ?
> Shall tribulation, or distress, or persecution, or
> famine or nakedness, or peril, or sword? As it is
> written for thy sake we are killed all the day long;
> we are accounted as sheep for the slaughter. Nay,
> in all these things we are more than conquerors
> through him that loved us. For I am persuaded,
> that neither death, nor life, nor angels, nor prin-
> cipalities, nor powers, nor things present, nor things
> to come, Nor height, nor depth, nor any other

creature, shall be able to separate us from the love of God, which is in Christ Jesus our Lord. (Rom. 8:35-39)

When the Son of man comes shall he find faith on the earth? I challenge you my dear Christian brothers and sisters: "Examine yourselves, whether ye be in the faith; prove your own selves. Know ye not your own selves, how that Jesus Christ is in you, except ye be reprobates?" (2 Cor. 13:5). Ask yourselves: "Has history taught us anything at all?" As the late Dr. Francis Schaeffer asked us, "How should we then live?"

May the grace of our Lord Jesus Christ continue with you always, Amen.

Appendix
ॐॐ ॐॐ

The Plan of Salvation

As it is said in the book of Psalms: "The heavens declare the glory of God; and the firmament sheweth his handy work" (Ps. 19:1).

Although you may have looked up into the heavens and seen all of God's handy work, this alone is not enough. To simply believe in a God is not quite enough. As it is said in the book of James, "Thou believest that there is one God; thou doest well: the devils also believe, and tremble" (James 2:19).

Although there may be those that tell you that there are many ways to get to know God, The Bible tells a different story. "There is a way which seemeth right unto a man, but the end thereof are the ways of death" (Prov. 14:12). But, Jesus says: "I am the way, the truth, and the life: no man cometh to the Father but by me" (John 14:6).

Why do we all need Jesus? Because of Adam's sin we were all born sinners. As the Bible declares: "Wherefore as by one man sin entered into the world and death by sin, and so death passed upon all men, for that all have sinned" (Rom. 5:12) (ref. Gen. 2:17, 3:1-19; Ps. 51:5).

God declared in His Word that there would be a penalty for sin.

"Behold, all souls are mine; as the soul of the father, so also the soul of the son is mine: the soul that sinneth, it shall die" (Ezek. 18:4). For the wages of sin is death (Rom. 6:23).

Because of sin, men are separated from God which causes death both physically and spiritually. "But your iniquities have separated between you and your God, and your sins have hid his face from you, that he will not hear" (Isa. 59:2). "And you hath he quickened, who were dead in trespasses and sins: Even when we were dead in sins, hath he quickened us together with Christ, (by grace ye are saved)" (Eph. 2:1, 5).

Even if you were not on drugs, or have been to jail or committed any other really bad sin, the Bible says: "As it is written: There is none righteous, no, not one. For all have sinned and come short of the glory of God" (Rom. 3:10, 23). So, there is absolutely no earthly way out from God's judgment.

But, the good news is: "But God commended his love toward us, in that, while we were yet sinners, Christ died for us" (Rom. 5:8). "For Christ also hath once suffered for sins, the just for the unjust, that he might bring us to God, being put to death in the flesh, but quickened by the Spirit" (1 Pet. 3:18). "For God so loved the world that he gave his only begotten Son that whosoever believeth in him should not perish, but have everlasting life" (John 3:16). "For God sent not his Son into the world to condemn the world: but that the world through him might be saved" (John 3:17).

What are we saved from? Judgment. Remember God said the soul that sins, it shall die. The physical death that is experienced by all human beings is because we were all born sinners, and we all have sinned.

Just as when someone breaks the laws of the land, there are penalties to be paid. In the courts of law a judge can render a judgment according to the merits of the case and the evidence presented to him. Because God is a holy and perfectly righteous judge, He judges us according to His standards. The problem with man is that we were all born sinners, and we all have fallen short of the glory of God. There is only one judgment that could be rendered to all humanity since Adam. Guilty.

We get a view of the great white throne judgment, found in the book of Revelation 20:11–15. All who were not saved (who didn't accept Jesus as their personal Lord and Savior) were cast into the lake of fire, forever and ever.

So God sent His Son into the world as the Lamb of God to take away our sins by dying the death that we should have died, and making full payment for our sins. God placed our sins on Jesus Christ, and in exchange placed Christ's righteousness on us. This brought us back in right standing with God so that we would be no longer separated from God our Father. (Rom. 5:1; Eph. 2:11-18; Col. 1:13-14).

Who can be saved? Anyone. The Bible says "whosoever believeth in him shall not perish" (John 3:16). He also says, "Him that cometh to me I will in no wise cast out" (John 6:37).

What must you do to be saved. Nothing. Jesus did it all for you. The Bible says, "For by grace are ye saved through faith, and that not of yourselves: it is the gift of God: Not of works, lest any man should boast" (Eph. 2:8-9).

You mean to tell me that our own righteous works won't get us into heaven? No, they will not. The Bible says, "Not by works of righteousness which we have done, but according to his mercy he saved us, by the washing of regeneration, and the renewing of the Holy Ghost" (Titus 3:5).

No man is justified by the works of the law in the

sight of God, it is evident. "For the just shall live by faith" (Gal. 3:11). "Neither is there salvation in any other: for there is none other name under heaven given among men, whereby we must be saved" (Acts 4:12).

Faith in God's only begotten Son Jesus Christ is the only way to be saved. For the Scriptures say, "But as many as received him, to them gave he power to become sons of God, even them that believe on his name" (John 1:12). Sonship is a result of being "born again." Remember as sinners we were dead in trespasses and sins, although we had already been born physically. But, since God is a Spirit, and we are sinners separated from God, a second birth (spiritual) is necessary to become a son of God. This is the "power" referred to in the Scripture above. Therefore you must be born again to enter God's kingdom (John 3:3-5).

What must you do to be saved?

Believe in the only begotten Son, Jesus Christ. For the Bible says, "Whosoever believeth [trusts and follows] that Jesus is the Christ, is born of God, and shall be saved" (1 John 5:1; Rom. 10:9-13).

Repent. In Psalms 34:18, the Bible says, "the Lord is nigh unto them that are of a broken heart, and saveth such as be of a contrite spirit." We must humbly come to the Lord realizing that we are sinners and that we cannot save ourselves from judgment for our sins. Then we realize that we must turn from our sinful ways to Jesus and humble ourselves under His Lordship (Luke 13:3; Acts 2:38).

Receive Christ as the Lord of your life. That means renouncing all evil affiliations or associations, and following Jesus' example as written in His Word, the Bible.

Accept His forgiveness of sins, His love and salvation, His peace and joy, and His Holy Spirit.

Finally, you must find a Bible-believing, Bible-teaching, Holy Spirit-filled church. God did not wish for us to be alone through our Christian walk. We need the support of our Christian brothers and sisters. Television and radio ministries are fine, but they will never take the place of fellowshiping one with another. As the prophet Jeremiah says, "And I will give you pastors according to mine own heart, which shall feed you with knowledge and understanding" (Jer. 3:15). "Not forsaking the assembling of ourselves together, as the manner of some is; but exhorting one another: and so much the more, as ye see the day approaching" (Heb. 10:25).

If you would like to be saved, here is a model prayer that you might consider saying. Saying a prayer alone won't save you because God looks on the heart; however, if you are sincere, the Lord won't forsake you. "Lord Jesus, I realize that I'm a sinner, and I realize that I cannot save myself from judgment. I believe that because you are the Son of God, you were sent into the world to die for my sins, and you did so on Calvary's cross. I believe that on the third day you rose again, and you have the power and authority to save me and grant me eternal life, because of your blood that was shed. Jesus, forgive me of my sins, wash me in your blood, and fill me with your Holy Spirit. I accept you as the Lord of my life, and I renounce all works of Satan; therefore, I repent of my sins. I ask you to lead and guide me as my personal Savior."

My friend, if you said that prayer and truly meant it, then the Bible says: "That if thou shalt confess with thy mouth the Lord Jesus, and shalt believe in thine heart that God hath raised him from the dead, thou shalt be saved" (Rom. 10:9).

Welcome into the kingdom of God, and I'll see you in the rapture.

More Good Books from Huntington House

Heresy Hunters:
Character Assassination in the Church

James R. Spencer

An alarming error is sweeping the Christian Church. A small, self-appointed band is confusing Bible-scholarship with character assassination. These *Heresy Hunters* fail to distinguish between genuine error and Christian diversity and turn on their brothers in an ungodly feeding frenzy. Jim Spencer suggests that the heresy hunters themselves might be the real heretics, because their misguided zeal risks splitting the church. He calls upon them to abandon their inquisition.

ISBN 1-56384-042-1 $8.99

The Extermination of Christianity—
A Tyranny of Consensus

by Paul Schenck with Robert L. Schenck

If you are a Christian, you might be shocked to discover that: Popular music, television, and motion pictures are consistently depicting you as a stooge, a hypocrite, a charlatan, a racist, an anti-Semite, or a con artist; you could be expelled from a public high school for giving Christian literature to a classmate; and you could be arrested and jailed for praying on school grounds. This book is a catalogue of anti-Christian propaganda—a record of persecution before it happens!

ISBN 1-56384-051-0 $9.99

Freud's War with God:
Psychoanalysis vs. Religion
by Jack Wright, Jr., Ph.D.

Freud's hostility to religion was an obsession. He dismissed religious belief as a form of mental illness—a universal neurosis. In this book, Dr. Jack Wright demonstrates the total incompatibility of the atheistic writings of Freud with Christian principles. His influence can be felt in such varied phenomena as: Gay Rights, Outcome-Based Education, and the False Memory Syndrome.

ISBN 1-56384-067-7 $7.99

Exposing the AIDS Scandal
by Dr. Paul Cameron

Where do you turn when those who control the flow of information in this country withhold the truth? Why is the national media hiding facts from the public? Can AIDS be spread in ways we're not being told? Finally, a book that gives you a total account for the AIDS epidemic, and what steps can be taken to protect yourself. What you don't know can kill you!

ISBN 0-910311-52-8 $7.99

Homeless in America:
The Solution
by Jeremy Reynalds

Author Jeremy Reynalds' current shelter, Joy Junction, located in Albuquerque, New Mexico, has become the state's largest homeless shelter. Beginning with fifty dollars in his pocket and a lot of compassion, Jeremy Reynalds now runs a shelter that has a yearly budget of over $600,000. He receives no government or United Way funding. Anyone who desires to help can, says Reynalds. If you feel a burden to help those less fortunate than you, read this book.

ISBN 1-56384-063-4 $9.99

Subtle Serpent:
New Age in the Classroom
by Darylann Whitemarsh
& Bill Reisman

There is a new morality being taught to our children in public schools. Without the consent or even awareness of parents—educators and social engineers are aggressively introducing new moral codes to our children. In most instances, these new moral codes contradict traditional values. Darylann Whitemarsh (a 1989 Teacher of the Year recipient) and Bill Reisman (educator and expert on the occult) combine their knowledge to expose the deliberate madness occurring in our public schools.

ISBN 1-56384-016-2 $9.99

Conservative, American & Jewish—
I Wouldn't Have It Any Other Way
by Jacob Neusner

Neusner has fought on the front lines of the culture war and here writes reports about sectors of the battles. He has taken a consistent, conservative position in the academy, federal agencies in the humanities and the arts, and in the world of religion in general and Judaism in particular. Engaging, persuasive, controversial in the best sense, these essays set out to change minds and end up touching the hearts and souls of their readers.

ISBN 1-56384-048-0 $9.99

How to Homeschool (Yes, You!)
by Julia Toto

Have you considered homeschooling for your children, but you just don't know where to begin? This book is the answer to your prayer. It will cover topics such as: what's the best curriculum for your children; where to find the right books; if certified teachers teach better than stay-at-home moms; and what to tell your mother-in-law.

ISBN 1-56384-059-6 $4.99

Out of Control, Who's Watching Our Child Protection Agencies?

by Brenda Scott

This book of horror stories is true. The deplorable and unauthorized might of Child Protection Services is capable of reaching into and destroying any home in America. No matter how innocent and happy your family may be, you are one accusation away from disaster. Social workers are allowed to violate constitutional rights and often become judge, jury, and executioner. Innocent parents may appear on computer registers and be branded "child abuser" for life. Every year, it is estimated that over 1 million people are falsely accused of child abuse in this country. You could be next, says author and speaker Brenda Scott.

ISBN 1-56384-069-3 $9.99

Loyal Opposition: A Christian Response to the Clinton Agenda

by John Eidsmoe

The night before the November 1992 elections, a well-known evangelist claims to have had a dream. In this dream, he says, God told him that Bill Clinton would be elected president, and Christians should support his presidency. What are we to make of this? Does it follow that, because God **allowed** Clinton to be president; therefore, God **wants** Clinton to be president? Does God **want** everything that God **allows**? Is it possible for an event to occur even though that event displeases God? How do we stand firm in our opposition to the administration's proposals when those proposals contradict biblical values? And how do we organize and work effectively for constructive action to restore our nation to basic values?

ISBN 1-56384-044-8 $8.99

Don't Touch That Dial:
The Impact of the Media on Children and the Family
by Barbara Hattemer & Robert Showers

Men and women without any stake in the outcome of the war between the pornographers and our families have come to the qualified, professional agreement that media does have an effect on our children—an effect that is devastatingly significant. Highly respected researchers, psychologists, and sociologists join the realm of pediatricians, district attorneys, parents, teachers, pastors, and community leaders—who have diligently remained true to the fight against filthy media—in their latest comprehensive critique of the modern media establishment (i.e., film, television, print, art, curriculum).

ISBN Quality Trade Paper   1-56384-032-4 $9.99
ISBN Hardcover 1-56384-035-9 $19.99

New Gods for a New Age
by Richmond Odom

There is a new state religion in this country. The gods of this new religion are Man, Animals, and Earth. Its roots are deeply embedded in Hinduism and other Eastern religions. The author of *New Gods for a New Age* contends that this new religion has become entrenched in our public and political institutions and is being aggressively imposed on all of us.

This humanistic-evolutionary world view has carried great destruction in its path which can be seen in college classrooms where Christianity is belittled, in the courtroom where good is called evil and evil is called good, and in government where the self-interest of those who wield political power is served as opposed to the common good.

ISBN 1-56384-062-6 $9.99

Journey into Darkness: Nowhere to Land
by Stephen L. Arrington

This story begins on Hawaii's glistening sands and ends in the mysterious deep with the Great White Shark. In between, he found himself trapped in the drug smuggling trade—unwittingly becoming the "fall guy" in the highly publicized John Z. DeLorean drug case. Naval career shattered, his youthful innocence tested, and friends and family put to the test of loyalty, Arrington locked on one truth during his savage stay in prison and endeavors to share that critical truth now. Focusing on a single important message to young people—to stay away from drugs—the author recounts his horrifying prison experience and allows the reader to take a peek at the source of hope and courage that helped him survive.

ISBN 1-56384-003-3 $9.99

When the Wicked Seize a City
by Chuck & Donna McIlhenny with Frank York

A highly publicized lawsuit . . . a house fire-bombed in the night . . . the shatter of windows smashed by politically (and wickedly) motivated vandals cuts into the night . . . All because Chuck McIlhenny voiced God's condemnation of a behavior and life-style and protested the destruction of society that results from its practice. That behavior is homosexuality, and that life-style is the gay culture. This book explores: the rise of gay power and what it will mean if Christians do not organize and prepare for the battle, and homosexual attempts to have the American Psychiatric Association remove pedophilia from the list of mental illnesses (now they want homophobia declared a disorder).

ISBN 1-56384-024-3 $9.99

The Media Hates Conservatives:
How It Controls the Flow of Information
by Dale A. Berryhill

Here is clear and powerful evidence that the liberal leaning news media brazenly attempted to influence the outcome of the election between President George Bush and Candidate Bill Clinton. Through a careful analysis of television and newspaper coverage, this book confirms a consistent pattern of liberal bias (even to the point of assisting the Clinton campaign).

The major media outlets have taken sides in the culture war. Through bias, distortion, and the violation of professional standards, they have opposed the traditional values embraced by conservatives and most Americans, to the detriment of our country.

ISBN 1-56384-060-X $9.99

Beyond Political Correctness:
Are There Limits to This Lunacy?
by David Thibodaux, Ph.D.

Author of the best-selling *Political Correctness: The Cloning of the American Mind,* Dr. David Thibodaux now presents his long awaited sequel—*Beyond Political Correctness: Are There Limits to This Lunacy?* The politically correct movement has now moved beyond college campuses. The movement has succeeded in turning the educational system of this country into a system of indoctrination. Its effect on education was predictable: steadily declining scores on every conceivable test which measures student performance; and, increasing numbers of college freshmen who know a great deal about condoms, homosexuality, and abortion, but whose basic skills in language, math, and science are alarmingly deficient.

ISBN 1-56384-066-9 $9.99

Trojan Horse—
How the New Age Movement Infiltrates
the Church
by Samantha Smith &
Brenda Scott

New Age/Occult concepts and techniques are being introduced into all major denominations. The revolution is subtle, cumulative, and deadly. Through what door has this heresy entered the church? Authors Samantha Smith and Brenda Scott attempt to demonstrate that Madeleine L'Engle has been and continues to be a major New Age source of entry into the church. Because of her radical departure from traditional Christian theology, Madeleine L'Engle's writings have sparked a wave of controversy across the nation. She has been published and promoted by numerous magazines, including *Today's Christian Woman, Christianity Today* and others. The deception, unfortunately, has been so successful that otherwise discerning congregations and pastors have fallen into the snare that has been laid.

ISBN 1-56384-040-5 $9.99

A Call to Manhood:
In a Fatherless Society
by David E. Long

Western society is crumbling—from the collapse of the family...to our ailing economic system, from the scandals in the church...to the corruptions in the Halls of Congress, from the decline of business...to the pollution of Hollywood, everywhere, we see moral and societal decay. The reason, says author David Long, is that the vast majority of men in America have received tragically inadequate fathering, ranging from an ineffective father to no father at all. This book presents a refreshing vision and a realistic strategy for men to recapture their biblical masculinity.

ISBN 1-56384-047-2 $9.99

A Jewish Conservative Looks at Pagan America
by Don Feder

With eloquence and insight that rival contemporary commentators and essayists of antiquity, Don Feder's pen finds his targets in the enemies of God, family, and American tradition and morality. Deftly . . . delightfully . . . the master allegorist and Titian with a typewriter brings clarity to the most complex sociological issues and invokes giggles and wry smiles from both followers and foes. Feder is Jewish to the core, and he finds in his Judaism no inconsistency with an American Judeo-Christian ethic. Questions of morality plague school administrators, district court judges, senators, congressmen, parents, and employers; they are wrestling for answers in a "changing world." Feder challenges this generation and directs inquirers to the original books of wisdom: the Torah and the Bible.

ISBN 1-56384-036-7 Trade Paper $9.99
ISBN 1-56384-037-5 Hardcover $19.99

Please Tell Me. . . Questions People Ask about Freemasonry—and the Answers
by Tom C. McKenney

Since the publication of his first book, *The Deadly Deception*, Tom McKenney has appeared on over 200 talk shows, answering tough questions about Freemasonry from viewers and audiences throughout the USA and Canada. Now, in his latest book, McKenney has compiled the questions most often asked by the public concerning the cult-like nature and anti-Christian activities of the Masonic movement. McKenney tackles topics, such as; Masonry's occult roots; Death Oaths and Masonic Execution; Masonry and the Illuminati; and Masonry's opposition to Christian schools. Tom McKenney warns Christians of all denominations to extricate themselves from Masonic movements.

ISBN 1-56384-013-8 $9.99

The Dark Side of Freemasonry
Edited by Ed Decker

In June 1993, a group of Christian researchers, teachers, and ministry leaders met in Knoxville, Tennessee, to gaterh together all available information on the subject of Freemasonry and its relationship to the Christian world. Their plan was to study the data that each would present on some facet of the Masonic problem and prepare a battle plan to stop Freemasonry from achieving its hidden agenda. Ed Decker has brought this explosive material back from Knoxville and here presents it as a warning to those who are unaware of the danger of the Masonic movement. The Masonic Lodge will never be the same after this book is released...and you will never be the same after reading it!

ISBN 1-56384-061-8 $9.99

Legalized Gambling—America's Bad Bet
by John Eidsmoe, Ph.D.

We are assured by the gambling interests that legalized gambling will provide tax revenue for the state, jobs, and prosperity for all. How should we respond to the lure of legalized gambling? Is gambling linked to organized crime? Does gambling create any new wealth? Does gambling prey upon poor people as a regressive form of taxation? John Eidsmoe takes us inside the casinos, the racetracks, and the halls of politics and law enforcement—unmasking the truth about legalized gambling.

ISBN 1-56384-071-5 $7.99

Hungry for God,
Are the Poor Really Unspiritual?

by Larry E. Myers

In God's eyes, there are no second-class citizens,
writes Larry E. Myers in this uplifting account of his
battle to put God, not ministerial success, at the fore-
front of his ministry. Inspired by the conviction that the
blood of Jesus is the great equalizer, Larry Myers set
out to bring much-needed hope and relief to the desper-
ately poor of Mexico. He believes—and *Hungry for God*
proves—that one man with a vision *can* make a difference.

ISBN 1-56384-075-8 $9.99

Resurrecting the Third Reich,
Are We Ready for America's Modern
Fascism?

by Richard Terrell

Is America ripe for a Holocaust of its own? According
to author Richard Terrell, there are frightening parallels between our own society and that of Nazi Germany.
Adolf Hitler and his minions deceived millions of decent
Christian people with propaganda that appealed to
their spiritual needs. That same strategy is being
employed today to lure Americans into worshiping the
false gods of the New Age movement and secular
humanism. With spreading cultural despair and scorn
for the Word of God among intellectuals, teachers, and
even ministers, we are closer than most Americans
realize to the utopianism that seeks to "cleanse" society.

ISBN 1-56384-019-7 $9.99

ORDER THESE HUNTINGTON HOUSE BOOKS !

_____	America: Awaiting the Verdict—Mike Fuselier	4.99	_____
_____	America Betrayed—Marlin Maddoux	6.99	_____
_____	Beyond Political Correctness—David Thibodaux	9.99	_____
_____	A Call to Manhood—David E. Long	9.99	_____
_____	Conservative, American & Jewish—Jacob Neusner	9.99	_____
_____	The Dark Side of Freemasonry—Ed Decker	9.99	_____
_____	Deadly Deception: Freemasonry—Tom McKenney	8.99	_____
_____	Don't Touch That Dial—Barbara Hattemer & Robert Showers	9.99/19.99	_____
_____	En Route to Global Occupation—Gary Kah	9.99	_____
_____	*Exposing the AIDS Scandal—Dr. Paul Cameron	7.99/2.99	_____
_____	The Extermination of Christianity—Paul Schenck	9.99	_____
_____	Freud's War with God—Jack Wright, Jr.	7.99	_____
_____	Goddess Earth—Samantha Smith	9.99	_____
_____	Gays & Guns—John Eidsmoe	7.99/14.99	_____
_____	Heresy Hunters—Jim Spencer	8.99	_____
_____	Hidden Dangers of the Rainbow—Constance Cumbey	9.99	_____
_____	Hitler and the New Age—Bob Rosio	9.99	_____
_____	Homeless in America—Jeremy Reynalds	9.99	_____
_____	How to Homeschool (Yes, You!)—Julia Toto	4.99	_____
_____	Hungry for God—Larry E. Myers	9.99	_____
_____	*Inside the New Age Nightmare—Randall Baer	9.99/2.99	_____
_____	A Jewish Conservative Looks at Pagan America—Don Feder	9.99/19.99	_____
_____	A Journey into Darkness—Stephen Arrington	9.99	_____
_____	Kinsey, Sex and Fraud—Dr. Judith A. Reisman & Edward Eichel (Hard cover)	11.99	_____
_____	The Liberal Contradiction—Dale A. Berryhill	9.99	_____
_____	Legalized Gambling—John Eidsmoe	7.99	_____
_____	Loyal Opposition—John Eidsmoe	8.99	_____
_____	The Media Hates Conservatives—Dale A. Berryhill	9.99	_____
_____	Out of Control—Brenda Scott	9.99	_____
_____	Please Tell Me—Tom McKenney	9.99	_____
_____	Political Correctness—David Thibodaux	9.99	_____
_____	Prescription Death—Dr. Reed Bell & Frank York	9.99	_____
_____	*The Question of Freemasonry—Ed Decker	2.99	_____
_____	"Soft Porn" Plays Hardball—Dr. Judith A. Reisman	8.99/16.99	_____
_____	Subtle Serpent—Darylann Whitemarsh & Bill Reisman	9.99	_____
_____	*To Moroni With Love—Ed Decker	2.99	_____
_____	Trojan Horse—Brenda Scott & Samantha Smith	9.99	_____
_____	When the Wicked Seize a City—Chuck & Donna McIlhenny with Frank York	9.99	_____

*Available in Salt Series

Shipping & Handling _____
TOTAL _____

AVAILABLE AT BOOKSTORES EVERYWHERE or order direct from:
Huntington House Publishers•P.O. Box 53788•Lafayette, LA 70505
Send check/money order. For faster service use VISA/MASTERCARD
Call toll-free 1-800-749-4009.
Add: Freight and handling, $3.50 for the first book ordered, and $.50 for
each additional book up to 5 books.

Enclosed is $_____including postage.
VISA/MASTERCARD #_____ Exp. Date _____
Name_____ Phone: (   ) _____
Address_____
City, State, Zip_____